Contents

SACRED ENERGIES

Forthcoming titles in

Sacred ✹ Energies

a series from Fortress Press in collaboration with
The Religious Consultation on Population,
Reproductive Health and Ethics

The Justice Men Owe Women:
Positive Resources from World Religions
John C. Raines

Power, Pleasure, and Justice
Mary E. Hunt and Patricia Beattie Jung

The Right to Family Planning
Daniel C. Maguire

SACRED ENERGIES

When the World's Religions Sit Down to Talk about
the Future of Human Life and the Plight of This Planet

Daniel C. Maguire

Fortress Press
Minneapolis

Cover art: "Canticle" by Mark Tobey, from the Smithsonian American Art
Museum; gift of the Sara Roby Foundation. Used by permission.
Cover design: Marti Naughton
Interior design: Beth Wright

Figure 1 on page 27, "Global Economic Disparities," is reprinted from Human
Development Report 1992, by United Nations Development Programme,
copyright © 1992 by United Nations Development Programme, and is used by
permission of Oxford University Press, Inc.

Library of Congress Cataloging-in-Publication Data
Maguire, Daniel C.
    Sacred energies : when the world's religions sit down to talk about the
future of human life and the plight of this planet / Daniel C. Maguire.
        p.   cm.
    Includes bibliographical references.
    ISBN 0-8006-3216-8 (alk. paper)
    1. Human ecology—Religious aspects. 2. Religion and social problems.
I. Title.
GF80 .M334 2000
291.1'78—dc21
                                                                00-056183

Manufactured in the U.S.A.   AF1-3216
04   03   02   01   00   1   2   3   4   5   6   7   8   9   10

1. The Wake-Up Call

POWER-HOLDERS OF THE WORLD, take notice!

The world's religions grew up rather separately. Even when they had some common Scriptures as Judaism, Christianity, and Islam did, they quickly parted and went their own ways. Any contact they had was often hostile, even to the point of war, pogrom, persecution, and crusade. In spite of that, they have this in common: they were all powerfully influential in the development of cultures, sometimes for good and sometimes for ill.

Now, in what is an almost unnoticed breakthrough in human history, the religions of the world have decided to sit down and talk to one another. No one even thought it possible. How could Hindus and Muslims, Confucians and Buddhists, Jews and Christians, and native religions of every stripe have a conversation together? They are not only talking; they are planning, strategizing, and forming alliances of conscience. They are interested in doing again what they have done in the past—changing the way the world thinks, acts, and does business—but now they are interested in doing it together.

Two-thirds of the world's peoples actively affiliate with the world's religions, and the other third cannot escape their impact on thought and basic attitudes. Anyone who ignores religion is ignoring a central force in our humanity and in the functioning of human society.

Religion, in a word, is power. John Henry Newman, a nineteenth-century British cardinal, said that people will die for a dogma, a religiously held conviction, who will not stir for a conclusion. Why is that? Religion is, quite simply, a response to the sacred. The word *sacred* is the superlative of *precious*. And there is nothing we take more seriously than that which we call sacred. So when all the religions of the

1

world, animated and charged as they are with a sense of the
sacred, start talking and bonding and planning together, history is about to turn a corner. An epoch is about to be born.

And why is this suddenly happening?

Fear.

Of course, not only fear. But fear is a big part of it. The
ancient Hebrews noted that fear is the beginning of wisdom.
Fear in the presence of danger is smart. Those who are fear-
less in time of danger just don't see the problem. Fear is like
pain in the presence of infection. It alerts you to the fact that
there is a problem and that you ought to do something about
it. And our lovely and lonely little planet is in danger. In all
the vastness of the universe, our earth may be the only one
that sprouted the miracle called life. Religion is the response
to life as sacred. Ethics is the response to life as good. Human
beings are the privileged bearers of religion and ethics. As
such, we have special obligations to the earth and to the life-
miracle of which we are a part, but neither religion nor ethics
seem to be up to the challenge of doing proper reverence to
the life that bore us. "It's a dumb bird that befouls its own
nest," goes an old saying. But *homo sapiens* (Latin for "wise
man"), as we have all too prematurely called ourselves, has
done just that.

Some, in fact, would say that we are the fatal flaw in the
evolution of life on earth. In richly poetic language, the great
anthropologist Loren Eiseley indicts humankind for wound-
ing the earth. He writes:

> It is with the coming of human beings that a vast hole
> seems to open in nature, a vast black whirlpool spinning
> faster and faster, consuming flesh, stones, soil, minerals,
> sucking down the lightning, wrenching the power from
> the atom, until the ancient sounds of nature are drowned
> in the cacophony of something which is no longer
> nature, something instead which is loose and knocking
> at the world's heart, something demonic and no longer
> planned—escaped, it may be—spewed out of nature
> contending in a final giant's game against its master.

That's pretty tough judgment on a species that has such a
high regard for itself. We have proclaimed ourselves the pin-

nacle of evolution! "A little less than the angels," the Hebrew
Scriptures call us. "What a piece of work!" says Shakespeare.
How dare Eiseley call us earth wreckers, "something demonic"
and cacophonic that is breaking the world's heart!

Before dismissing Eiseley's grim view of us, a chastening
look at some of the ominous new facts of life should bring
blushes of guilt to the faces of those who fancy themselves
stewards of the earth. Reader, be warned. It is no easier to
look at the facts I will give here than it is to look at the sun.
But squint a little and dare to look at these realities.

Bad News

We depend on cropland and on the earth's generous waters.
Topsoil, that precious and thin layer of life support, is wash-
ing like blood into the seas and rivers, blowing away in the
wind, and getting paved over. Over a period of thirty years,
China, where one of five humans lives, lost in cropland the
equivalent of all the farms in France, Germany, Denmark,
and the Netherlands. Of the earth's vegetated surface, 43
percent is to some degree degraded, and it takes from three
thousand to twelve thousand years to develop sufficient top
soil to form productive land. On a typical day on planet
earth, 71 million tons of topsoil are lost. If we were losing
huge quantities of gold, it would be a lesser tragedy.

Oysters are another witness to earth woes. The oysters do
for seawater what our kidneys do for us. They purify it and
filter the water as they feed themselves. The fabled Chesa-
peake Bay once enjoyed a thorough filtration by the massive
oyster population every three days. Thus cleansed, the bay
flourished. It was fish heaven. Now, the oysters are so deplet-
ed that the filtration occurs only a few times a year with por-
tentous results. Similarly, mussels, as they busily take in vast
quantities of water to glean out microscopic plankton, perform the filtering process for inland waters in the United
States. Seventy-seven percent of them are either extinct or
endangered.

The major rivers of the heavily populated nations are all
polluted. Remember that less than 1 percent of the earth's
water is safe to drink. Life grew on earth because it is the

water planet. And yet we are busily poisoning this most precious of resources. Potable water is not evenly distributed on planet earth. Most of Africa, the Near East, northern Asia, and Australia are on the short end of water supply, and they suffer from chronic water shortages. Water wars are already in the offing. Notice that negotiations between nations in the Middle East are beginning to talk more of water than of oil.

The seas were the original source of life, and they have been since the beginning of the earth a generous mother. Yet the richness of the seas is spoiling like the land. Of the seventeen major world fisheries, nine are in decline, and all the others are threatened by unsustainable fishing practices. As far as the analysts' eyes can see into the future, we are faced with declining supplies of fish per person. Indeed, per capita supplies of water, fish, meat, and grain are declining. The world's grain harvest is now regularly below consumption, drawing down grain stocks to the lowest level on record. Any shopper knows that means steadily rising costs of grain, and the hungry know that that means more hunger.

Until recently, we thought the world was infinite. We wanted all poor nations to develop so they could live like we do. Now we know that only about three billion people could eat a typical American diet, and there are over six billion of us on earth. We know too that if China were to eat fish at the same rate as Japan does, it would require the entire fish product of the earth. In a word, there are limits to what the earth can produce. If everyone ate like we eat and consumed goods like we do in affluent countries, it would take many earths to meet the supply. This one is too small.

Not surprisingly, in solidarity with the dying earth, people are dying too. When it comes to impoverishment, the rule seems to be, "Women and children first!" Four million babies die yearly from diarrhea in the euphemistically named developing world. Next come the women. Dr. Noeleen Heyzer of the United Nations says, "Poverty has a female face." Women constitute 70 percent of the world's 1.3 billion absolute poor, and *absolute poverty* means you do not have the basic necessities of life. In parts of Africa, only 18 percent of the people have access to clean drinking water. Seventy percent of the children in upper Egypt suffer from water-related diseases. It has been said that if one glass of pure water was the cure for AIDS, most people in the world would not have access to it. Every year, up to sixty million people die from hunger-related causes, and over a billion people lack the calories for an active working life.

Microbes and viruses that found a life for themselves in the forests have accepted deforesting humans as their new hosts. As population expert Joel Cohen says, "The wild beasts of this century and the next are microbial, not carnivorous." More than thirty new diseases have been identified since 1973, many of them relating to our new and ecologically dangerous lifestyles.

Meanwhile, there are more of us. It took ten thousand generations to reach the first population of 2.5 billion; it took one generation to double it. Till the middle of the next century, the momentum is unstoppable. Overall fertility rates have been declining over the past forty years, but mortality rates are dropping even faster, and so our numbers inexorably grow.

World population is like a triangle, with the reproductive young at the wide base and the old at the narrow top. Until the model comes closer to a rectangle, with a more balanced distribution of young and old, the growth will not stop, nor does anyone expect it to.

A new Mexico is added almost every year; a new China every twelve years. And over 90 percent of the growth is in the poorest parts of the world. The United States is in no position to lecture the rest of the world on this. At the current rate of increase, we add a Connecticut every year and a California every ten years.

The results of all this earth wrecking do not stay overseas. Try as they may, affluent nations cannot become gated communities hidden safely away from the pollutions of poverty. The results of ravished ecologies overseas come home to us. Those poisons arrive in air, water, and strawberries. Acid rains fall on the affluent and the nonaffluent alike. Professor David Orr of Oberlin College gives us some of the scary data: male sperm counts worldwide have fallen by 50 percent since

1938. Human breast milk often contains more toxins than are permissible in milk sold by dairies. At death, some human bodies contain enough toxins and heavy metals to be classified as hazardous waste. Toxins delivered during pregnancy affect the immune systems of newborns, the most innocent of the innocent. Almost 80 percent of European forests have been damaged by acid rain. Fifteen years ago, I was driving through the Black Forest in Germany and a sign hung by the road, announcing *Der Wald Stirbt!* "The forest is dying!" And so it is. And these are just some of the sad tidings of our failed service to this generous host of an earth.

Sixty-five million years ago, a barrage of asteroids hit this planet, ending the life of all the dinosaurs and almost ending earth life. Scientists say that a comparable threat is now hitting the planet. This time, it's not asteroids. It's us.

Stop! This is too much bad news. Why did I buy this book, you may be asking, if it is just going to depress me!

Stay! Don't leave me yet. To pick up a pen, said Albert Camus, is an act of hope, and I have picked up the pen. This book is out to offer two *h*'s: humility and hope. And if hope does not have the last word, you can write to me and demand a refund.

Acts of Hope

Humility, however, sounds like more bad news. It's not. Once understood, it's a lovely word. It is a dose of realism, and realism is always ultimately more refreshing than illusion. *Humility* comes from the Latin *humus,* meaning "earth" or "soil." We rise from the earth and return to it. As eco-theologian Larry Rasmussen puts it, "Even the molecules in our face and body are there only temporarily on their journey to and from the environment." There is nothing demeaning about humility, about realizing that our lives—like those of the mallard, the cornstalks, and the rose—emerged like miracles from the humus. It is even more stunning to go back further in our lineage and realize that we, the mallard, the corn, the rose, and even the humus of earth resulted from a star-burst that spewed out the planets of our solar system. In the truest sense, the cells of our bodies are made of stardust.

We are children of the universe. Earth life, all of it, is a community with common roots in stardust. No drama conjured by human minds can match that for grandeur and surprise!

Admittedly, we are gifted children in the earth-life cast. We're smarter than the cows and the hippopotami, which makes us both glorious and a threat, but we are not supreme or independent. We are an afterthought in the history of life on earth. The rest of nature, on which we absolutely depend, was here for billions of years without us. It's humble and truthful to recognize that. And it is humbler yet to realize that the rest of nature did well without us and could do well without us again. Ecologists point out that earth life could dispense with humans and thrive; it is the crawling, creeping things like insects, spiders, worms, snails, and protozoans that earth life cannot do without. If they left, life on earth would be reduced to a mess of scroungy algae and bacteria. But if we were to disappear, the birds would still be on the wing, and the flowers would greet unpolluted springtimes with unimpeded extravagance. As far as the rest of nature is concerned, we would not be missed.

And we really could and might disappear. The dinosaurs survived some 200 million years. We should go to the museum and bow before their replicas. If our present habits continue—as seen in the gloomy data given above—we will never match their record for survival. We have been here in some kind of an identifiable form for two million years, but if current trends continue, we will not. Vaclav Havel, the president of the Czech Republic, says the earth will not indulge our abuse forever: "If we endanger her, she will dispense with us in the interests of a higher value—that is, life itself." Lynn Margulis, the microbiologist, is even more blunt. She says very matter-of-factly that the rest of nature did well without us before we came, and it will do well without us when we are gone.

So the essential virtue of humility says we should glory and revel in the beauty of life on earth—ours and that of the rest of the earthly life community—but we should know that we can forfeit our citizenship in this biological community. The human species thus far has been a typical adolescent. As with all adolescent rebels, we have pretended to an independence we do not have, and, like all bratty kids, we have no sense of what we owe to what went before us. It's grow-up time.

The hurtful side of ecological humility is the experience of limit after a long period of pretending we had none. The sweet side is a Franciscan sense of oneness with all of nature, all the other children of humus, and the parental sun. From the sun that energizes all life to the fauna and flora around us, we are family. The family is not all good. There are lethal viruses and cruel diseases. The salmon that becomes the bear's lunch or ours learns that violence is built into the life cycle. The life that is good also bears the mark of the tragic. And yet, happily, beyond all the horrors of the world, there are the first smiles of infants, the undefeatable growth of greenery from volcanic ash, the ingenuity of evolution, the historic realization of many bold dreams, the beauty of heroic minds and sunsets and human love. The yes is mightier than the no. Joy is at home in our universe.

And so humility, a true experience of our reality, gives birth to hope, and my promise is to deliver hope.

Thoughtful people have noticed all of the destruction our aberrant species has inflicted on our earth home, and they want to do something about it. Many of these thoughtful people are experts and leaders in world religions. They realize that all religion is born of reverence, reverence for the miracle of life in all its forms. All the great religions of the world are epics of wonder. They are driven by a profound sense of justice and compassion. They are all enemies of egoism and exploitation. They all house dreams of a flourishing earth. They come at these things in different and fascinating ways, and we will look at these enchanting differences in this book. We can visit the often surprising variances in attitude toward a number of basic realities. They define sacredness in different ways, some by talking of a god or gods, some with no god at all. Each is a classic of what we now call spirituality. Some are better than others in understanding our relationship to the rest of nature. All of them arrive at a sense of human solidarity. Not all believe in an afterlife, but all address the meaning of suffering and attitudes toward the poor, and all of them dream of peace. Each of them is chock-full of ideas that relate to issues that we call today feminism, human rights, and moral obligation. Their insights can also fit right into modern discussions of sexuality, population, and depopulation. These are classics of human thinking well worth tapping.

None of these religions is a complete success story. They all contain terrible stuff. As they gathered their pearls of wisdom, they also dragged along the refuse of the centuries. Students of religion must learn to reject the damaging refuse that accumulated in every religion and go for the pearls. Remember too that some of these ancient religions did not even think of themselves as religions. Some did not even have a word for religion in their vocabularies. They all thought of themselves, however, as philosophies of life. They all thought that what they were struggling to develop and speak could shape what we call the politics and economics of the world around them. Like the travelers in *The Canterbury Tales,* each of the religions of the world has a story to tell about life as it is and life as it can be. And each of those stories has hope for the human race and for our endangered home. We have nothing to fear and everything to gain from hearing one another's stories. It is these stories of hope that will fill these pages.

This book had its origin in a particular happening. With support from the Ford Foundation and the John D. and Catherine T. MacArthur Foundation, some of us formed a group with the long name of the Religious Consultation on Population, Reproductive Health and Ethics. We gathered some of the best scholars from the world's religions and brought them together to discuss the plight of our damaged world. They represented the religions presented in this book. Many people think those religions are dead and useless. Many are sleeping giants, but in their day they all turned their societies upside down. Lately, they haven't done much of that. Since the eighteenth-century Enlightenment, they have been sidelined and sidetracked. But they are not dead, and they can rise again. In this project, we spent days together—

Native Americans, Hindus, Buddhists, Jews, Muslims, Christians, and Taoists—searching for the renewable moral energies of these rich traditions and applying them to problems of ecology, population, and the greed of overconsuming societies. The experience was exhilarating.

As in this book, we began with two of the best international critics of the global economy, David Korten and David Loy. Both are experts on global economy and its impact on our ecology. Before looking into our particular religious and moral traditions, we wanted to face the facts of political and economic life on planet earth. Only after listening to them will we begin the tour of those forces that we call the religions of the world.

Each chapter will have one or two principal tour guides. The scholar who worked with us from each of the religions and professions will lead us, but I will bring supplementary witnesses into our journey. The goal is to join the powerful currents of thought represented by these scholars and to do so in understandable language. Scholar-babble will be avoided like poison. There are ideas here that can save the world and save those quarter of a million children who die every week from malnutrition and infection. The power and relevance of these traditions should not be hidden in elitist or pompous jargon.

Open your mind humbly and hopefully, and join us on the tour. Remember, the next two chapters are going to be amazingly interesting—and a little scary—tours conducted by economic philosophers. You would expect that to be dull and boring. It won't be. It contains the facts of life that many business leaders and politicians hope the common folk never learn. Then we will see what the religions have to say about the mess we are in.

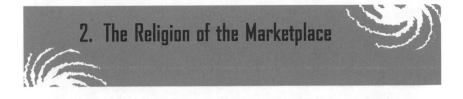

2. The Religion of the Marketplace

THE GREATEST SEDUCTION IN THE HISTORY OF THE WORLD is well under way. Almost all the nations in the world are being sold a batch of snake oil that the charlatans tell us will cure all our ills and bring us happiness. The more we gulp it down, the worse we feel; we and our children and our surroundings are becoming more poisoned. And so we gulp some more. It might be smarter to stop and think for a moment.

Snake Oil

David Loy is our principal tour guide in this chapter. Loy is a philosopher who gives special attention to economics, but don't let that put you off. One jokester said that if you took all the economists in the world and laid them end to end, it would be a good idea. Don't do that to David Loy. He is a penetrating thinker who makes sense and is possessed of a beautiful and sensitive conscience. A native-born American who now lives and teaches in Japan—and teaches in Japanese—he is also a practicing Buddhist. He travels the world lecturing and studying, and he has reached some remarkable conclusions.

He has studied that very snake oil that most of the world is now drinking, the economic system that is called capitalism, free enterprise, and often now the global marketplace. He doesn't say that capitalism in some form should or is going to disappear. But he points out that in its current form, it is the grand imposter. It is playing a role for which it has no talent. It's making like a religion. It is doing the things that religions have traditionally done: telling us what is sacred, what is valuable, and how we should behave. What's more, it is doing all these things even more effectively than the religions did in their heyday. This "religion of the market," Loy says, is on its way to becoming "the first truly world religion, binding all corners of the globe into a worldview and set of values." Through its enormous advertising outreach, it is doing what the missionaries of old could never do. It penetrates every hamlet and village from Bangladesh to Donegal. It has, says Loy, "already become the most successful religion of all time, winning more converts more quickly than any previous belief system or value system in human history."

The religion of the market, as Loy calls it, is not recognized as a religion because it wears secular drag. It even presents itself as rationalized by a science called economics. However, Loy says, "the discipline of economics is less a science than the theology of that [consumerist capitalist] religion, and its God, the Market, has become a vicious circle of ever-increasing production and consumption by pretending to offer a secular salvation." Money is so much God that people refer to this religion now as "moneytheism."

An economic system as a religion is nothing new. Money from its very beginnings has always been tied up with religion. The temple was the first mint. The coins made there were consecrated by the priests, and this made them valid currency. In fact, the very word *money* comes from the name of a Roman goddess, Moneta, also known as Juno. It was in her temple that the first Roman coins were made. Money's nature seems to give it a link to the gods. As economic analyst William Greider observes, money contains an "illusion of immortal power." Though we are not sure we will survive death, we know our money will. It extends our control beyond the grave. So economic systems are easily linked up with religion. When the United States dropped the gold standard in 1933, conservative Republican Representative Bill Dannemeyer said it was a violation of "formal rules from God through the vehicle of the Bible." It is no shock, then, to hear David Loy's opinion that our current form of capitalism is functioning like a religion. It is shaping our minds with its edicts and dogmas, just as religions have always done.

Meanwhile, back at the other religions, what is going on? The religions that used to be the main culture makers and value givers are being supplanted—even overwhelmed—by this new belief system and value system that has simply swept them aside. Though Loy has great hopes for the religions as power sources that can spark revolutions in consciousness, he sees most of them as slipping into irrelevance. "The major religions are not yet moribund but, on those few occasions when they are not in bed with the economic and political powers that be, they tend to be so preoccupied with past problems and outmoded perspectives that they are increasingly irrelevant (e.g., fundamentalism) or trivialized (e.g., television evangelism)." At times, he says, they seem, if not dying, at least senile.

Any hope for them?

Yes, Loy says, the current ecological disaster, some of the details of which I gave in chapter 1, might stir these massive giants from their torpor. When the first Earth Day was celebrated in the United States about thirty years ago, many viewed it as a left-wing sideshow. We are more alert now. The poisons are reaching our kitchen tables and fast-food counters, and ecological awareness is reaching new heights. As Loy says, it is showing us "that we need a deeper source of values and meaning than market capitalism can provide," and it is also making us admit that contemporary religions are not meeting this need well. The new interest in spirituality, which is the word most moderns now like to use for religion, is a signal of discontent. The sense that something is wrong is growing, but we are still getting sucked in by the very forces that are seducing and destroying us and producing the havoc detailed in chapter 1.

The industrial revolution was not so much a new way of making things as it was, in the words of French historian Fernand Braudel, "a transformation of desires, . . . a revolution in demand." Its success depended on making us *want* more things than we ever could *need*. And it does this with a mind-altering tool, the likes of which had never been seen before. It is called advertising.

Consumerism on the Rampage

In 1994, just as an example, the United States spent far more on advertising than on all of higher education—$147 billion! This money ground out 21,000 constantly repeated television commercials; millions of magazine advertising pages; 14 billion mail order catalogs; 38 billion junk-mail ads; and a billion signs, posters, and billboards. On top of all that, another $100 billion went into promoting fashion. The onslaught is stupendous, enough to turn our brains to mush. Worldwide, $450 billion are spent annually on advertising, enough to end all hunger and to create decent employment for everyone who is able to work.

The defenders of this rogue form of market capitalism would stop us here and say, Hold on! Without the advertising, the market would grind to a halt, and everybody would lose his or her job. This advertising onslaught, they would say, is essential to the system. If we keep doing things the way we are doing them now, of course, these defenders of status quo capitalism are right. Capitalism as now arranged—there are other ways of doing it—is built on a double greed: the greed for profits and the greed of consumers. Consumerism is the fire that drives the engine. If we don't keep buying, they can't keep producing. Corporations are not built on kindness or love. They may make a gesture here and there to social and ecological values but, to remain competitive, their only passions have to be profit and growth. That is the nature of the beast as it now exists. And so the propaganda advertising barrage is endless, now even reaching into our elementary schools as corporations buy rights to advertise in the school buildings themselves! And it works. We are on a rampage of consuming that is staggering.

According to the Worldwatch Institute, more goods and services were consumed between 1950 and 1990 than by all the previous generations in human history. The problem is that we are asking more of the earth than the earth has to give. The earth just cannot keep supporting our consumerist habits.

But, some reader might object, for all its faults, maybe this system is not so bad. After all, look at the mess the communists made trying to do it another way! And those formerly communist countries are now rushing to do it our way.

That is true and false. True, communism made a lot of messes. Clearly, we don't want to imitate those messes. But it is false to imply that our form of capitalism is making no messes and that it needs no serious overhaul.

But before looking at its messes, we have to look squarely at the first dogma of the religion of the market. That dogma is inevitability. There is a temptation in every religion to decide that outside that religion there is no salvation. Medieval Christians used to say *extra ecclesiam nulla salus,* "outside the church there is no salvation." Consumerist-driven capitalism says the same. Only capitalism—as we now do it—can save us; the collapse of communism is the latest proof of that.

Here is where David Loy the economist and David Loy the Buddhist meet. Buddhism is centered on the idea of our need for enlightenment. The assumption is that we are freighted with a false consciousness that kills our awareness of alternatives. We become prisoners of the status quo, of the way things are, and we castrate our capacity to dream dreams of liberation or improvement.

Take an example of this from the past, because it is easier to appreciate the stupidities of the past than our own on-going stupidities. In the early years of the eighteenth century, some dreamers who were thought a little strange by all the sensible and realistic people of their time decided that human beings could do away with kings and found a democracy. The wilder ones of them imagined that there could be representative government that could be voted in and voted out, that there could be a balance of powers in the government so that no one part of it might become a new form of royalty. Crazy ideas and quickly rejected as such by most people. After all, there have always been kings, and that is just the way it is. (Most people get caught in the paralyzing belief that what is has to be.)

Then all of a sudden toward the end of the eighteenth century, a group of people in what is now the United States decided that those ideas were not crazy at all, and they actually put them into effect. Their bold minds were so sure about the allegedly crazy ideas that they even said, "We declare these truths to be self-evident," etc. They dared to reimagine society. Thomas Paine wrote in his famous tract

Common Sense in 1775: "We have it in our power to begin the world over again. A situation similar to the present hath not appeared since the days of Noah until now. The birthday of a new world is at hand." They didn't buy the inevitability dogma of royalty. No wonder Ben Franklin and the other early American fellows were the toast of Europe. They did it! They dared to rethink human life and to imagine new forms of politics and economics.

Reimagining Our World

It is time for a new reimagining. The challenge today is to reimagine our society. And at this point, I begin to feel weak, and my courage is stretched to the breaking point because most people buy the inevitability dogma. "If it ain't broke, don't fix it," the saying goes. The news they need is that it is "broke," and it does need fixing.

While not forgetting the comforts and joys that capitalism has brought to many of us, here are the problems that the "inevitable-ists" need to face. Here is why we need to be as bold as the founding leaders of the United States. We need their courage to think of better ways.

These are some of the messy results of consumerist capitalism, results that hurt all of us.

Dogma number one: price determines value. One cynic said that today we know the price of everything and the value of nothing. Our capitalism holds it as dogma that price determines value. That means that if something does not have a price, it does not have value. You don't have to be an economist to realize that value ought to determine price. You should pay what something is worth. Turning that upside down is a dumb mistake, and dumb mistakes in economics tend to hurt a lot of people and our good earth. The ecological disaster that is poisoning our bodies, waters, and fields comes from the false economic belief that nature is an "externality." Our economics did not put a price on it, so mainstream economics treated all of nature as worthless. It doesn't compute when you are figuring out costs. So you poison Lake Erie and the local air. No problem. Air and water are externalities—no price, no value. Now green environmental movements are challenging this, pointing out with former U.S. Senator Tim Wirth that "the economy is a wholly owned subsidiary of the environment."

But scorn of Mother Nature is still enshrined in the temple of the market. The young and still-feeble environmental movement has not disenthroned it. In fact, corporations are rushing from countries that protect the environment to nations where there are no such laws or where the laws are not enforced, so they can merrily pollute away! Of course, the mess they make there comes back home to us in the strawberries and hamburgers we import, and in the rain and in the air. Pollution does not respect borders. On top of that, when the polluters move, they take your job too, which brings us to the second mess of the market religion.

Dogma number two: labor is a production cost to be minimized. That is not the way you read about it in the newspapers. "Downsizing," "Shifting to Part-Time Workers," "Move to Workerless Factories"—that's the way it makes the headlines. In today's market thinking, laborers or the workforce have some value, but it is the price that hurts. If you value profits over people, then it adds to the bottom line to sack workers or open a sweatshop south of the border or in inner cities to cut down on worker costs. If you think of people as costly things and not as persons marked by the sanctity of life, you can make more cash by unloading as many of those things as possible. Between 1980 and 1993, the Fortune 500 firms increased their assets almost two and a half times, but they shed 4.4 million jobs. Meanwhile, surprise of surprises, compensation for CEOs—chief executive officers—increased more than sixfold to an average of almost $4 million a year. The more pink slips for the workers, the more greenbacks for the managers. At the same time, unions are getting weaker as American workers have to compete with workers in Latin America and Asia who are working for slave wages. And the managers love the decline of unions, one of the few forms of clout that workers have left.

More good news for the managers is on the way: automation. Technology is inventing machines to replace people. And machines are great. They don't take coffee breaks or sick leave, and they don't go on strike or form unions, and they don't cause you trouble by sexually harassing one another. In the United States, in the past thirty years, the number of factory workers has declined from 33 percent of the workforce to under 17 percent. Meanwhile, overall production has increased. Within ten more years, that 17 percent will shrink to 12 percent; by the year 2020, fewer than 2 percent of the entire global workforce will still be engaged in factory work. The blue-collar, mass assembly-line worker is on the way out.

In the past, when agriculture mechanized, and fewer workers were needed, the factories took up the slack. As factories went robotic, the service industries—banking, insurance, wholesale, and retail sectors—stepped in. Now, guess what? The service industries are automating, replacing the white-collar workers, but there is no place for displaced service workers to go.

Lessons from Europe

The situation is not hopeless. It is only hopeless if you buy the so-called wisdom of the market that places no value on human life and the need of human beings to be productive and creative. Jeremy Rifkin, who writes on this move to "workerless factories" and "virtual companies," shows that companies that decide to treat workers as persons and not as discardable commodities can meet the new demands. Hewlett Packard in France and BMW in Germany have reduced their workweeks to thirty-one hours with no reduction in pay. In return, the workers have agreed to work in shifts, thus keeping the high-tech plants operating on a twenty-four-hour basis, which increases productivity. They are thus paying the workers more to work less, and productivity is going up.

European workers are rallying around the cry, "Work less, work all." This means they want a thirty-five-hour workweek, or even a thirty-hour workweek, so that there will be jobs for more people.

This might work. Even greedy managers know that unemployed people don't buy their products. High employment and low unemployment are ultimately better for business. This is not a new idea.

In England, for example, after World War I, the workweek was reduced from fifty-four hours to forty-eight or even forty-six to absorb the influx of returning military personnel. This move kept unemployment low and wages high.

In France, government officials are considering rescinding payroll taxes for the employer if management reduces the workweek. Robert Reich, former secretary of labor in the United States, has suggested tax breaks for companies that do not downsize but look for creative alternatives to keep faith with their workforce. Rifkin suggests that the federal government ought to extend tax credits to any company willing to do three things: (1) reduce its workweek, (2) implement a profit-sharing plan so that the employees, and not just the managers, benefit from increased productivity, and (3) restrain top management and shareholder dividends to a proportionate and reasonable level so that the workers get a fair share of the benefits of increased productivity.

The cancer that is eating away our prosperity is called the military budget. Rather than spending $30 million an hour on military spending now as the United States is doing (while we arguably need less than half of that to meet any and all military needs), we should invest that military welfare money in education. With just a fraction of the military pork, we could triple the number of elementary and high school teachers and double their salaries to produce the finest schools in the world. The wealth of the future is in ideas. That is where we should be investing. We should also invest in the environment, creating industries that reap the pure and infinite power of the sun and the wind. We should invest in the arts and in health care. We should invest in U.S. trains, which are pathetically out of date. Trains running to 190 miles an hour race up and down Germany, France, and Japan. Our trains can hardly stay on the tracks; when they are on the tracks, they lumber along at 1950 speeds. Beautiful, spacious, job-making trains could traverse our land and allow us to travel in comfort, without long airport waits. Much work remains to be done and millions of needs to be met,

once we stop thoughtlessly raping the earth to feed our con-
sumer habit and making bombs that only the bomb makers
need.

   None of this will happen until people of conscience demand
respect for all persons and the right of all persons to meaning-
ful work. None of this will happen until we defeat the second
dogma of consumerist capitalism, which treats workers like a
drain on profit and not like persons with sacred human rights.

   As we will see further in this book, the world's major religions condemn this kind of thinking. You cannot be a good
Buddhist or Christian or Jew or Muslim or Hindu and think
this way and treat people this way. One thing all the world's
great religions have in common is reverence for life, for the
life of people and for the rest of the life that fills the earth.
The kind of global capitalism that has been developing since
World War II is dumping people and destroying nature. As
far as all the religions of the world are concerned, this capitalism is a heresy.

   So what is the ultimate answer to the objection, Communism failed; capitalism is the only answer. The answer is, Yes,
communism failed, and our global capitalism is also failing.
All the statistics given at the beginning of this chapter illustrate that failure. It takes our jobs, poisons us, impoverishes
us, shifts wealth from the bottom to the top—making wars
of redistribution more likely—and it encourages terrorism
since not everyone is willing to play by the rich deal makers'
rules.

   A recent cartoon pictures a father, mother, and three children seated around the kitchen table. A number of bills are
scattered across the table. The father announces, "Because
of inflationary pressure, I am going to have to let two of
you go."

   This cartoon is funny because that is not what people do
in a family. In a household, when times are tough, you find
new modes of sharing. You don't let anyone go down the
tube. The religions of the world see the human family as a
household, and they all teach that the essence of morality is
to see that everyone gets what it takes to live. Our new market religion blesses the power of money to drive to destitu-

tion those poor nations that used to be able to feed themselves. Rather than planting to feed themselves, they plant so-called cash crops that go to support the well-off in the affluent pockets of the world, leaving their own people literally starving. This is encouraged by powerful transnational corporations that have grown bigger than most countries and have the power to bully governments and people with impunity. Our next tour guide, the distinguished economist David Korten, will give us lessons on what happens when corporations rule the world.

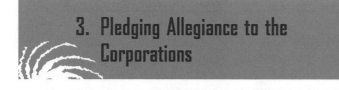

3. Pledging Allegiance to the Corporations

PEOPLE USUALLY TAKE NOTICE OF REVOLUTIONS: the French Revolution, the Russian Revolution, the American Revolution. We are right in the middle of a revolution that makes those revolutions look paltry, and most people are looking the other way. Nation-states that developed over recent centuries, with their constitutions and bills of rights, are diminishing in power and being replaced by other entities. The corporations are replacing them, and very few people seem to even notice this. Of the one hundred biggest economies in the world, more than fifty are not nations but corporations.

It used to be that the biggest economies in the world were nations. There were companies in these nations, some big, some small, but they were never a match for the nation-state. The effects of this revolutionary shift of power from nations to the corporations are massive and, for poor folks, often lethal.

Nations and their governments had to be tamed, and it wasn't easy. We had to get rid of the divine rights of kings and the idea that the king could do no wrong. We fought over the centuries to civilize national governments, to democratize them, to equip them with systems of law and due process including constitutions and bills of rights. The corporations are new, and we have had no time to tame them. Too few Patrick Henrys have arisen to cry tyranny at the unrepresentative power of corporations as they grow so big as to dwarf most nations. How did all this happen?

David Korten, like David Loy, our gentle guide in the last chapter, is an economist. But like David Loy, he talks sense, and normal folks can understand him. David Korten is a Patrick Henry. He is challenging corporate tyranny. He is the paramount expert on the reshaping of the world that took place successfully at a place called Bretton Woods.

"In the Beginning . . ."

Back in 1944, a group of men sat down and decided to write the script for the post–World War II world. And by *world* they meant the whole world. The place they met was Bretton Woods, New Hampshire, and the decisions they reached affect every one of us every day. They affect our job security, our confidence in the safety of our food and our water, and our attitudes toward the world. These men decided that the various national economies should be global, not local. They formed institutions that most people have heard about, but are afraid to really look into because they are so far away and complicated, and most explanations of them are full of unintelligible gobbledygook. Economics, yuck! The World Bank, the International Monetary Fund (IMF), the World Trade Organization (WTO)—who could ever understand them?

David Korten does, and he tells us about them with straight talk. Is he some sort of an antibusiness radical? No. He admits to "the depth of [his] conservative roots." His résumé shows him at the heart of what we call the establishment. He was a captain in the Air Force during the Vietnam War, then taught at Harvard's business school, and worked for years for the United States Agency for International Development. He believes in a market system and in the right to private property. He distrusts big government, but he also distrusts big business, especially when huge corporations get the power to overwhelm governments and begin to devastate both people and the environment, answering to no one. No conservative or liberal could like that!

And here is why David Korten fits so tightly into our journey in this volume. He is the peer of any economist in analyzing our world situation. He is also fully aware of all the human and ecological disasters that I listed in chapter 1. And he feels that the crisis can be solved only by tapping into the collective wisdom of the world's religions. Our crisis, he says, is not just economic or political. More charts and graphs by economists will not solve it. The human crisis today is spiritual. People have lost contact with their spiritual roots, and with the reverence and compassion inspired by those classic spiritualities and moral masterpieces that we call world religions. Korten himself was raised as a Protestant Christian, but he finds great and relevant wisdom in all the world's religions; he pleads with religious people to listen to an analysis of the world's economic and ecological plight and then to repair to the treasuries of religious wisdom in our collective effort to save the world. Societies, in his view, are held together by "a shared sacred meaning."

Now, with Korten as our prime mentor, surprise yourself, gentle reader, and see how easily you can understand the grand ideas that have shaped our global economy. This is the stuff the power-holders don't want you to know, and it is not nuclear physics.

The Bretton Woods fellows meant well. They were meeting in 1944 after the fall of Mussolini and with Hitler's demise only ten months away. They were filled with hope for a postwar world of peace and prosperity, and they designed the institutions that they thought would make it happen, the World Bank and the IMF, and they laid the foundation for what would become the WTO to handle international trade and tariffs. The purpose of these institutions, according to Henry Morgenthau, the U.S. secretary of the treasury and president of the Bretton Woods Conference, was the "creation of a dynamic world economy in which the peoples of every nation [would] be able to realize their potentialities in peace and enjoy increasingly the fruits of material progress." This is a sweet vision, and who could object to it?

But, alas and alack, these experts made two whopper mistakes: First, they assumed that the richness of this planet is such that economic growth would know no limits. Morgenthau was agog with optimism. He declared this earth of ours "*infinitely* blessed with natural riches" (emphasis added). He exultantly took it as an "elementary economic axiom . . . that prosperity has no fixed limit. It is not a finite substance to be diminished by division." Thus spake Morgenthau in 1944, and none spoke in disagreement. This hallucination, however, continues. Move into the 1990s and listen to Lawrence Summers, former chief economist of the World Bank before becoming undersecretary of the treasury in the Clinton administration: "There are no . . . limits to carrying capacity of the Earth that are likely to bind at any time in the foreseeable future. . . . The idea that we should put limits on growth because of some natural limit is a profound error." This is, dare I say, a bit crazy. Every day the worldwide economy burns an amount of energy that the planet took ten thousand days to create. There are finite limits to coal, natural gas, and oil, and renewable sources like wood are being clear-cut out of existence. Remember the statistics given above that the planet could support fewer than three billion people eating a typical American diet. There is not that much to go around. You don't have to be a brain surgeon to know that there are limits to growth. The planet on which we live has limits, and we are approaching them.

And yet these powerful agencies, the World Bank and the IMF and the WTO, were all born of the illusion of infinity. You have to admit that that was a huge and fatal flaw.

But now to the second and very painful flaw in the design of our current global economy. The Bretton Woods designers assumed that global trade would benefit all peoples and that the rising tide really would raise all boats and give boats to those who didn't have them. The word *development* grew out of this Bretton Woods faith. The world would consist of developed nations, that is, industrialized nations where everyone was well-off, and developing nations, where everyone was on the way to being industrialized and well-off. Here is wondrous naïveté. Let's tease out its errors.

First of all, if everyone was as industrialized as the United States is, we would all choke to death. And where would we get the raw material for all that industry? As more and more nations get developed in this sense, we are beginning to read of excessive production, with more cars and other items being produced worldwide than there are customers for them. The word *deflation* is suddenly appearing in business journals as merchants realize that products are outnumbering customers. And as more and more nations get developed, we begin to read of them choking to death. As I have just said, the IMF and the World Bank have led the charge in getting all people developed.

When Thailand followed their script, the directors of these two organizations decided to meet in Bangkok in 1991 to taste firsthand the fruits of their vision. Bangkok was once a beautiful and charming city. If the directors could have seen beyond the shining shopping malls, the high-rise office buildings, and the luxury hotels, however, they would have seen a disaster. Bangkok is one big traffic jam. Three hundred thousand new vehicles are added to its streets every year, slowing traffic to an average of six miles per hour! On more than two hundred days a year, the air is intolerably polluted. Emissions are still increasing by 14 percent a year. Huge slums and squatter settlements surround the high-rising symbols of success.

Development? Good news for the poor? Hardly.

The Bretton Woods thinking was a grand example of self-serving trickle-down posturing, the kind whose slogan might well be, "Let the greedy have their way and the overflow will trickle down to the poor." This ignores the fact that the greedy are master plumbers who can plug all possible holes so that little if anything will trickle down to anyone.

At the core of the Bretton Woods silliness was the conviction that globalization was salvation, salvation for everyone. Turn the massive corporations loose, open all borders to trade, and poor people will be just fine. As an antidote to this nonsense, these fellows needed a little dose of what Christians and Jews call original sin, an insight into the selfishness and coldness that blights human hearts and human society, or a little of the enlightenment that Buddhists seek. The major religions of the world are experts on the weaknesses and strengths of the human heart. They specialize in this. Their voices were needed at Bretton Woods, and they weren't there.

In the whole history of the world, very few planners were as successful as those who sat in Bretton Woods to sketch the future of the world. They actually got the main lines of their vision turned into reality. However, the product did not match the rosy portrait they painted for themselves in 1944. Today, poverty is worse, and obscene wealth is commonplace. Money is roaring to the top.

Notice the graph provided by the United Nations Development Program. The top 20 percent of the world owns 82.7 percent of the world's income; 17.3 percent is left for the remaining 80 percent of the world.

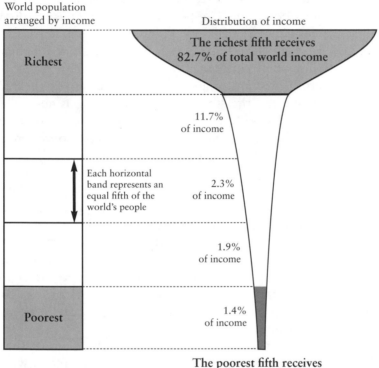

World population arranged by income

Distribution of income

Richest

The richest fifth receives 82.7% of total world income

11.7% of income

Each horizontal band represents an equal fifth of the world's people

2.3% of income

1.9% of income

Poorest

1.4% of income

The poorest fifth receives 1.4% of total world income

FIGURE I

Globalization became a new rubric for exploitation. In the post–World War II world, corporate giants roamed about the planet seeking the cheapest resources and labor they could find and looking for dumps for their wastes. As we know, the corporate soul, unchecked by conscience, has only two passions: profit and growth. The first question asked in executive boardrooms around the world is never, How will this help the poor? Indeed, the very thought of that should bring cynical smiles to the least cynical among us!

What globalization has done is produce a "big sucking sound" (to borrow Ross Perot's term). The powerful nations and corporations suck what they need out of the weak and the poor. Japan, for example, is powerful enough to get rid of what it does not want. Copper-smelting plants are a dirty nuisance. So Japan financed the Philippine Associated Smelting and Refining Corporation to do the dirty work for them in the Philippine province of Leyte. An impoverished Philippine government expropriated four hundred acres of land from the poor, and the smelting plant was in business. The result? Gas and wastewater emission containing high levels of boron, arsenic, heavy metals, and sulfur have contaminated local water supplies, reducing fishing and rice yields, damaging forests, and increasing various diseases among the local residents. The local people compete for the smelting plant's most dangerous and dirty jobs. The company has prospered. The Japanese people have a supply of copper at no environmental cost to themselves. The local people have lost their means of livelihood and suffer impaired health. At the same time, Japan imports more than 50 percent of its wood from the rapidly disappearing rain forests of Borneo. That's the way global capitalism, operating without a conscience, is working out.

Wealthy nations behave like bullies, taking more than their share. If you were to visit the Netherlands tomorrow on a decent budget, you would feel they are at the same level of affluence as the United States. This is amazing when you realize they would need fourteen times the amount of land they have to live as well as they are living. How do they do it? They buy it out of other nations, the poorer nations. As David Korten puts it, the deficits of the industrialized nations are largely covered by "trade that allows them to expropriate the resources of lower-income countries."

Old-fashioned imperialism used to have to move into these countries with gunboats and an army. The corporations just buy their way in, create a rich local elite who enjoy it, but wreck the ecology of the nation and the formerly self-sustaining economy of the poor. Some boats rise, and most sink. Each nation seizes the opportunity to create its own champagne class (see figure 1, p. 27) with a bloated upper class and a huge underclass.

The logic of the globalizing economy—pushed and financed by the World Bank and the IMF and the WTO—which treats both poor people and the environment as raw material to be exploited, is brutal. It has forced poorer countries to use their resources to sell to the powerful. Thus, millions of small farmers in Brazil who used to be able to feed themselves peacefully were pushed off their land so that cash crops for export could take their place. To feed the growing appetite for meat by the elite of the world, export cattle ranches in Latin America and southern Africa are replacing rain forests and wildlife ranges and small farms where people used to be able to feed themselves. The earth's ecology and its people are devastated by this.

In India, big development projects that were supposed to make everyone well-off displaced twenty million people over a forty-year period. In Mexico, a million families will be displaced from their farms as a consequence of the North American Free Trade Agreement. According to David Korten, World Bank staff have been unable to point to a single bank-funded project in which the displaced people had been successfully relocated with a standard of living comparable to what they enjoyed before displacement!

Can you see why David Korten can say that the World Bank and the IMF "have arguably done more harm to more people than any other pair of nonmilitary institutions in human history"?

Strong talk. But he makes a compelling case that they should be dismantled and that institutions sensitive to people and ecology should be created. It can be done, but not until people see the problem and push for a solution.

Gated Communities

It is not that this new world has not brought great benefits and progress. Cures for diseases keep people living longer—though this varies greatly depending on your access to good nutrition and medical care. Prehistoric persons lived on the average, factoring in infant death, eighteen years. In ancient Greece, the figure was twenty years; in ancient Rome, twenty-two years. In medieval Europe, the average length of life was less than forty years, and in North America at the beginning of this century, forty-seven years. We have conquered diseases such as smallpox and polio, and even in the poor countries, life expectancy has increased by 33 percent over the past thirty years, with infant mortality rates cut in half. This could lead to the conclusion that in spite of all the problems, all of us, the rich and the poor, are really better off.

That blithe judgment writes off the more than one billion people today in absolute poverty, a fancy way of saying they are in the process of starving. Our medical advances mean little or nothing to them. In effect, we have treated them as compost for our gardens.

But how safe are our gardens? The ancient Jews saw that fear can be the beginning of wisdom. We should be afraid. Corruption and pollution do not stay overseas. The dispossessed rise up in the only kind of war they can manage: terrorism. Environmental refugees—a new category—flood into cities and nearby countries. Development refugees—another new category—displaced from their self-sufficient farms to make room for smelting factories and cash crops, run to overcrowded cities. Such overcrowded cities rank second only to nuclear bombs in their capacity to pollute.

The rich nations are not immune to this earth wrecking. David Korten points out that countries with high income levels are experiencing increases in rates of cancer, respiratory illness, stress and cardiovascular disorders, birth defects, and falling sperm counts. He notes the research that attributes this to air and water pollution, to the chemical additives and pesticide residues in our food, high noise levels, and increased exposure to electromagnetic radiation. "The poverty of the poor is their ruin," said the Book of Wisdom. The new lesson is that their ruin quickly becomes ours. Rich and poor, we're in this mess together. Suddenly, people are willing to pay more money for organic or natural food. *Organic* and *natural* mean that it is less likely to poison us.

Still on the bad-news side, Korten notes that our communities are unraveling. The word *neighborhood* means less and less. Job insecurity is rising. Ten years ago, 75 percent of Americans felt secure in their jobs; today, only 51 percent do. The number of workers employed by temporary agencies has increased 240 percent in ten years. Manpower, the largest of these, is now America's largest private employer. Not surprisingly, there are increased incidences of depression, divorce, teenage pregnancy, violence, alcoholism, drug abuse, crime, and suicide.

Any Hope Out There?

The good news about all of the above is that "it ain't necessarily so." Globalization that turns once-independent peoples into dependents does not have to be.

First of all, it is not that complicated. There is a wise old saying that if you want to get anything done, you should do two things: first, clarify your ideas; second, get friends. First, study the situation with confidence in your own intelligence, and find out the facts. If you are still reading this book after all the bad news I have given you, you are already doing the first part. Next step: take those ideas and join in with those who are doing something about it. Get your synagogue, mosque, or church moving on it.

Remember, Lyndon Johnson got elected in a landslide before people understood the futility of the Vietnam War. Three years later, in 1961, when they had caught on, he had to drop out before the race started. When the first Earth Day was celebrated in 1971, it was thought to be a sideshow, involving long-haired kids and some well-meaning Audubon ladies. But in just a few years, *Time* magazine would name the imperiled earth as the main story of the year. The U.S. government created the Environmental Protection Agency, and laws began to be passed to stop pollution, contrary to the wishes and lobbying of the big polluting corporations. In 1992 in Rio de Janeiro, the largest gathering of heads of state, political leaders, corporations—yes, corporations!—and citizen organizations in human history took place to work on agreements to protect the global environment. When people wake up, things happen. The demonstrations against the WTO in Seattle in 1999 were a sure sign of awakening.

Once again, the status quo is not inevitable. Without firing a shot, the people of the Philippines threw out the dictator Fernando Marcos in 1986. Who could have predicted that? As David Korten says, in 1988, anyone who dared to say that by 1991 the Soviet Union would peacefully dissolve itself would have been considered insane. Who could have predicted that the successors of that Soviet Union would now be inviting the United States to help dismantle its nuclear arsenal? Who could have predicted that Nelson Mandela would be elected the president of South Africa in an open multiracial election in 1994? In Korten's words, we quickly forget "how rapidly impossible dreams are becoming accomplished fact."

Corporations have no power that we do not give them. They are monsters that we made. When the United States was founded, the word *corporation* referred to an entity that was chartered by the state to perform certain functions for the common good. Cities, churches, and colleges were examples of corporations. Their main purpose signaled by a state charter was to serve the common good. In the nineteenth century, a fateful change happened. Legislatures started to sell charters for a fee with the stipulation that they behave themselves; that is, they had to obey certain organizational regulations. Gradually, the courts began to treat corporations as persons who could compete in the marketplace with other persons like you and me. What a mismatch! And, of course, thoughts of the common good went down the tube.

This was precisely what the founding fathers did not want. They were afraid of "economic royalists" and "private governments." They did not want to get rid of King George III and end up with King General Motors or Czar Microsoft. They wanted to tame government with a system of balance of powers. They did fairly well at that. They did not foresee the huge corporations becoming international powers balanced by nothing. The American Revolution was precisely a grand human effort to check unrestrained power. If we stand by in silence, the corporations will defeat that revolution. Corporations are beginning to control everything, TV and the newspapers, book publishers, and universities. As economist Paul Hawkin, a modern Paul Revere, puts it, "corporations achieve precisely what the Bill of Rights was intended to prevent: domination of public thought and discourse."

Corporations can't be eliminated. They are part of the economic landscape. But they don't have to do what we are letting them do. If people insist on it, corporations can be, to use a newly popular word, "conscientized." They can be controlled by the conscience of the people. David Korten's book *When Corporations Rule the World* (Kumarian Press, 1995) is chock-full of practical ideas for change. Korten favors a twenty-hour workweek as part of a way of keeping jobs in an automating world. He favors laws which could be passed immediately allowing workers or communities to buy out manufacturing plants that the corporation is trying to move out of a community. This would mean that when a corporation wants to close a plant or undertake a sale or merger, the affected workers and community should have the first legal right to buy the assets on preferential terms. These terms would reflect the workers' years of investment in labor for that company and the community's support of that company. Companies should not be allowed simply to pull anchor and sail into the sunset as though they had no debts to the community and to the workers who made them successful.

Korten urges the creation of new jobs directed at what he calls "the social economy." As factories automate, there is still plenty of work to be done, most of it a lot more interesting and challenging. Korten's social economy includes work like this: care for children and the elderly, educating young people, counseling addicts, providing really proper care for the mentally ill, maintaining parks and commons and extending them, organizing community social and cultural events, registering voters, cleaning up the environment, replanting forests, doing public interest advocacy, working on community gardens and recycling centers, retrofitting homes for energy conservation, teaching music and the arts to people who can't afford lessons. There are millions of good things to be done. Diverting even a part of our military spending would make them possible.

I hope these suggestions of David Korten—and these are just a few of them—have caught your attention. Buy his book *When Corporations Rule the World,* and make it the topic of your book club or religious discussion group. It is a hope-filled book along with being a scorching analysis of the way we are doing things now. Catch the excitement of seeing the possibilities of a new age. There is nothing more energizing than people power.

And there is nothing that could energize the sleepy old religions of the world faster than applying their dormant wisdom to all of this. All these religions in their origins were exhilarating revolutions in thought and feeling. And remember, Korten and other technically skilled economists realize that the motivation to renew our world in a joyful, thriving way can only come from a reborn sense of the sanctity of life. Scientists agree. A 1972 book produced by a study group at the Massachusetts Institute of Technology, *The Limits to Growth,* saw the disaster pending for the human race and concluded, "Probably only religion has the moral force to bring about [the necessary] change." Life on this earth is a miracle. We are the conscious part of that life. It is ours to save and enjoy or to squander. In 1990, thirty-four renowned scientists issued "An Open Letter to the Religious Community." In it they said, "Efforts to safeguard and cherish the environment need to be infused with a vision of the sacred." This book is one effort to respond to their call. Now we turn to some of the world's visions of the sacred.

If you are still reading, you have learned that you are smart enough to learn how economics works.

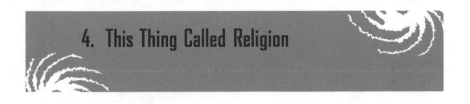

4. This Thing Called Religion

THE WITTY GEORGE BERNARD SHAW ONCE SAID that every profession is a conspiracy against the laity—that is, against those who are not part of the profession. Conspiracies are hostile things, and part of the hostility of the professions is to develop a language that only the "in" folks can understand. Doctors can be accused of this. If you had an enlarged liver and spleen, they could call that an enlarged liver and spleen, but they don't. They call it *hepatosplenomegaly*. That's a great name for it if you are Greek since in that language *hepatos* means "liver," *splenos* means "spleen" and *megaly* means "big." But in English, enlarged liver and spleen would do nicely. Most economists and philosophers are guilty of the same nonsense with their pompous technical jargon and weird charts, and yet we just met a philosopher and an economist, Loy and Korten, who rank at the top of their fields but can also speak English and speak it plainly. That's fine, and we thank them.

Now we are turning to another field, religion. Professionals here are usually called theologians, and let's face it, they have been just as guilty of obscurity as any other professional. The Buddha or Jesus or Muhammad can teach a simple and beautiful doctrine, but hand it over to the theologians, and who knows what is going on!

Buddhism, for example, began with refreshing insights marked by a lovely simplicity. It sought to cope with sorrow by taking a middle course between self-indulgence and extreme self-denial so as to lead a well-ordered and harmonious life. As A. J. Basham puts it, however, "This very simple doctrine was developed in various rather pedantic forms, most important of which was the 'Chain of Dependent Origination' . . . commented on again and again by ancient and modern scholars, and probably not fully understood by anybody."

Buddhist pedants were not alone. Christian speculations on the subsistent relations of the Trinity were far from the straightforward moral thunder of the prophets or from the powerful simplicity of Jesus' Sermon on the Mount. When it comes to unnecessary obscurity, none of the religions is without sin. The French have a saying that should guide us. Freely translated, it goes like this: "If you understand it clearly, you can say it clearly." So in the spirit of that saying, let us turn to this thing called religion and see what it really is.

Before we even try to define it, we can say that whatever religion is, it is powerful. Recall Cardinal Newman's observation that people will die for a dogma who will not stir for a conclusion. A dogma is a religiously held belief. The French philosopher Albert Camus said something like that when he noted that people will not die for scientific truth. It is only when they sense a value that they can call sacred that people can be fully devoted. And that gives us our clue as to what religion is.

Religion is the response to the sacred. That response can take a whole number of forms, and obviously the world is full of different—very different—religions. However, if they really are religions, if they really are responses to what we experience as sacred, they all have the same source and starting point.

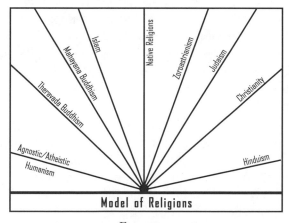

FIGURE 2

Figure 2 illustrates the origin of all religions. Notice that in this chart, all the religions start from the same point. I call it

Point Wow. That sounds a little irreverent, but it is not. All religions start with an experience of the wonder and grandeur of life on this planet. People see the flight of the dove and the explosions of beauty as flowers come to blossom. They marvel at sunsets and babies and even the genius of insects going about their business. They experience love, the supreme miracle of life, and what else could they say to all of the above but Wow! That expletive is the root of the word *sacred*. This life into which we were mysteriously born makes us all talk about the sanctity of life whether we are theists, atheists, or agnostics. The term *sanctity of life* is usually applied only to human life, but it goes further than that. The whole biological marvel from which we sprang has a sanctity about it and merits our reverence.

Wonder, said Aristotle, is the beginning of philosophy. Wonder is also the beginning of religion. The wonder, the reverence, the awe that we find in the miracle of life on this precious planet of ours perched in a privileged corner of this stunning universe is expressed in that primeval "Wow!"

So all religions are, at root, appreciative responses to the miracle of life. At the level of Wow, they are all siblings, born of the same parental delight. Then these religions take off on their separate cultural journeys through history, illustrated in the chart by the lines going out. As they move out, their imaginations spawn new symbols to express their ongoing experience of the Wow. Their histories shape their expression of religion and, as a result, they become very different from one another. Some explain life through monotheism—the idea that there is one creator God behind it all. Others are polytheists, believing in many gods. Some are not theistic at all, having no concept of God, and yet they are filled with reverence for life and compassion for all that lives. Buddhists, for example, are usually not theistic. They have a deep sense of the sacred and a reverence for life, but they don't believe in a god. Diversification is a rule of life, and religions are alive . . . and quite diverse.

But then the problem arises: how can we all get together to save and enjoy this earth if we are all so different?

The answer is to go back to that point where we can all be one, to Point Wow. That initial reverence and gratitude that birthed our religions and that still pulses at the heart of all religions is an experience open to everyone.

That's why it is not surprising that religions, diverse as they are, can come together in discussions of human rights and issues of ecology. Dogmas may differ, but reverence for life is our common ground. And that is enough for interreligious conversations on the huge problems that confront us all. We might also, as these interreligious conversations proceed, visit one another's dogmas and find enrichment there. As can be said of religions, if you know one, you know none. Religions need to enlighten one another. Together, we can bond in grateful appreciation of the glories of the life that came to us as pure gift.

Common Concerns

As we move through the various religions, which usually developed without communication with one another, it is surprising to see how they came to deal with the same human problems. As we go on to meet the various religions in subsequent chapters, we'll see how each of them tackled the problems we complex humans present. None of these religions is perfect or uncontaminated by the culture in which it grew up. All of them imbibed some of the poisons of their ambience. If that is all that they did, if they were just sponges absorbing all the meanness around them, they would be worthless. But all of them are interesting because they broke free from their surroundings. They struggled with our weaknesses and sensed our potential strengths. For that reason, they deserve a hearing. All of them. Each of them had some breakthroughs in wisdom. Each of them touched on problems we have to solve if we are to survive and thrive on this half-wrecked planet. Here are four of the problems that all religions tackle:

1. All religions consider egoism and an absence of any sense of *the common good* and human solidarity.

2. While calling it by different names, all the religions come up with some notions of what *justice* is and what *human rights* are, as well as what it means to *own* something. (We all might think we know what the word *owning* means, but wait and see.)

3. All religions get into the question of *status*. In doing this, they get into the question of how to treat those who are *poor and disempowered,* those who, in a proud world, have the lowest status. Though all the religions have sinned against women, they all have something relevant to say about the low status of *women* in most societies. The status question also applies to the rest of biological nature. All of these religions contain an attitude toward plants, animals, and the rest of the universe. Though they often stress human issues, they are not unaware that we are kith and kin to the rest of nature.

4. And, finally in this incomplete list, they all believe that life is not just a matter of survival, but also, to coin a word, of "thrival." If we are just surviving and not thriving, we are not really surviving at all. Each in its own way, the religions reached the conclusion that *joy and celebration* are our destiny. We are not meant to be scratching desperately for a meager subsistence. Efficiency and productivity are not all there is to life.

Probably the toughest problem on that list is the first one, egoism and selfishness, and all the religions go after it. That makes sense. The problems there affect all the other three areas on our list. Before moving to the various religions, we'll concentrate first on how egoism corrupts life.

Ants and Humans

As smart as we humans are, we have a radical fault, one that could almost make us envy the insects. I was speaking in Greece a few years ago to a group of Ford Foundation officers. I spoke of the common good, and at the end of my opening statement, we took a break. One of the officers asked me to explain when I resumed what the common good is. I took a walk down the path to the beautiful Aegean Sea. On the way down the path, I thought I saw a long black ribbon stretched across the path in front of me. When I got close, I saw that it was not a ribbon but two rows of ants going in opposite directions. Those going one way were all carrying something; those going the other were on their way back for another load. Obviously, a change of real estate was going on. The ants were moving.

What struck me was that their sense of the common good, of common needs requiring cooperation, was genetically inscribed. Their ethics was in their genes. It is not so with us. We are not genetically programmed to cooperate for our common good. We seem to be quite well programmed to look out for number one. We seem almost genetically selfish.

What is it in us that supplies for the genetically controlled cooperation of the insects? The answer is ethics. The answer is also religion, since all the religions we will study here are moral enterprises.

All of them are concerned with this human weakness of selfish disregard for the common good, perhaps the fatal flaw of our otherwise talented species.

I-Self or We-Self

The original sin of our modernity is what is called *individualism*. It had its birth in a good idea, that is, that the individual person should not be crushed under group considerations. It said to the state and to other social powers, "Don't tread on me." And that was good. It got carried too far, however, and we have lost our sense of being one human family living on a rich but limited earth. All the world's religions have lessons on how to keep the original good of individualism or personalism but regain our needed sense of being together and interdependent. Life on earth is a shared glory. Recovering our we-self consciousness—to know and feel our relatedness with all persons and with all that lives on this earth—is not only a release from loneliness but also the recipe for a flourishing earth.

Our guide here is professor Harold Coward of the University of Victoria in beautiful western Canada. Dr. Coward, a Christian himself, is a world-renowned expert on other religions. He has worked especially on Hindu-Christian relations, but his work takes him into conversations with most of the world's religions. His genius is outreach, and his forte is respect for the traditions of others. In a systematic way, he has brought together representatives of the world's religions and gotten them working together on the problems of this troubled earth.

Harold Coward gives us a warning about how many of us Westerners who live in North America and Europe have a special problem with egoism. Westerners are big on individual rights, and that is not all bad. In fact, it has done a lot of good. Precisely because of that stress on individual rights, poor people, people of color, and women—all of whom suffered from a dominant majority—have often led the way in asserting their rights. But there is also a danger for us Westerners. We can be more aware of what we are owed as individuals than of our obligations to the common good. As Coward says, this individualistic mind-set leads to "a concentration on rights rather than obligations." What you owe me crowds out what I owe you and everybody else . . . including what I owe the rest of nature.

In Coward's language, we in the European and American West are socialized into thinking of ourselves in an isolated way, as an I-self, as essentially segregated from others and very separate and distinct from the rest of nature. This is a lonely sense of self. It lessens our awareness of our obligations to other living humans on this small planet and to future generations, as well as to the rest of nature of which we are a part. Other cultures and the religions that grew up in them don't see it that way. They don't think of themselves in such an isolated, segregated, and lonely manner. Jewish, Islamic, Hindu, Buddhist, Chinese, and Aboriginal societies have a different, more social, more family sense of self. The concept of self is more of a we-self than an I-self.

Pause on this a moment, because Coward is leading us here on a journey into a land that might seem very mysterious to us. We could be put off by its foreignness. To help us see what he is saying, Dr. Coward uses some practical examples. The first is rather amusing. It occurred to him when he was a young professor of world religions. He knew a lot about those religions and had taught university courses on them. He found out a little more when he went to a conference with a Hindu professor. When they arrived at the hotel where they were sharing a room, he started to get an experience of the we-self in action. It became clear that since they were rooming together, his Hindu friend assumed they would do everything together—eating, going to sessions, taking a walk. With Western colleagues, roommates usually see one another only at the end of the day, with both following their separate interests very independently. With this Hindu colleague, Coward felt he was being merged into a shared identity and was no longer an autonomous individual. It reached extreme levels when Dr. Coward saw his colleague using his—that is, Dr. Coward's—toothpaste! The sense of ownership was definitely different. Any Westerner would see in this an invasion of one's privacy. This gentleman did not, nor would he have found it unusual if Dr. Coward had used his toothpaste. (Coward did not!)

The purpose of this story is not to suggest that this is the ideal way of sharing. There are good antiseptic reasons to keep our toiletries to ourselves. It does, however, illustrate the different view of self. Without idealizing it, it gives us grounds for some helpful comparisons. Right away, you might begin to wonder how this Hindu would react to other people's needs and problems. If you were in trouble, would you be better off in a we-self society? Before we try to draw any conclusions from all this, a few more examples will help us to get the picture of this cultural difference.

Coward, ever the good teacher, offers us other examples. His wife, Rachel, is a nurse who works in a family care unit in Canada where most of the patients are aboriginals. She discovered immediately that when a young woman or older teenage girl would arrive with gynecological problems, she would never arrive alone. Her mother, her aunts, and her grandmother would all come with her, and all would insist on going back to the examining room together! When the doctor started to take a history of the patient, the grandmother would do all the talking, right down to details about the girl's last period, etc. All of the women present knew everything. They all worked from a we-self concept, and they all expected to be involved in the treatment and in any ethical decisions to be made regarding that treatment.

What Rachel realized right away was that issues of *consent*, so important in medical ethics, would be quite different here since the consent in question would be a group activity.

Once again, I am not saying that this is the ideal to which we should all aspire. This could lead to a submerging of the individual into the group. When our son Tom was seven years old, he had a slight turn in his eye. The doctor spoke to Tom's mother and me in Tom's presence and suggested surgery in which he would delicately scrape the eye muscles in hopes of straightening the eye. We told the doctor we would get back to him after we had time to think about it. However, as soon as we left the office, little Tom looked up at us and said emphatically, "Nobody is cutting my eye!" I said to Rachel, "That's it; the decisions has been made." (Actually, the eye straightened out on its own later.)

So, putting Rachel's experience together with Tom's, we see something good in both. There is strength in the group experience of the aboriginal peoples. They think in terms of group interests. And there is strength in Tom's sense of himself. It was, after all, *his* eye, not his mother's or mine, and so we honored his decision.

As always, the answer lies in balance. We can honor Tom's right to bodily integrity, but we can also take instruction from the aboriginals. We I-self people have had less sense of the common good. We have, in Dr. Coward's words, been prone to "self-centered selfishness." It is easier for us to cut ourselves off from other people and also to cut ourselves off from the rest of nature. The aboriginal peoples of North America, being we-self people, did not take nature for granted. They knew that the "we" of we-self included Mother Nature, on whom we are totally dependent. Their respect for other animals and plants made them natural conservationists. They wept when they saw how the white folks tore up the earth.

Harold Coward speaks of the Anabaptist Hutterite attitude toward dying. Again, we see the we-self at work. A patient, Paul, was gravely ill with lymphosarcoma, or cancer of the lymph nodes. To get him the best treatment, he was taken from his colony to a hospital in the city where, because of distance and visiting-hour limits, his people could not be with him. He was transferred home when the treatments failed, and he died within a few hours. The community was devastated. The death, they said, was "too quick." As Coward puts it, "Paul's isolated time in hospital represented a lost opportunity for the collective self of Paul and his community to prepare a good death." There was no time to put his we-self to rest. The dying was too solitary, unlike his life, which was always communitarian. He died like an I-self, not like the we-self he had always been.

So the problem with the I-self culture that most of us Westerners were born into without even having had a vote is isolation. We will relate to others but from a safe center of isolated loneliness. I-selves have a tilt toward detachment and segregation. The word *segregation* comes from the Latin *grex,* meaning "group," and *sine* meaning "without" or "outside of." I-selves are inclined to define their interests selfishly, outside of the group and its interests. This, of course, is artificial and unreal because the good of the group is the setting for all individual good. Where there is no common good, there is no individual good. Our real interests have to be defined with an eye to the good of society at large and the good of nature of which we are a part. I-self thinking is an isolation illness. The isolation-ill patient loses contact with everything outside the self, and this we recognize as a sad sickness. I-self society loses contact with everything outside itself—including the air, water, and topsoil we require to live, and the result is societal sickness.

Harold Coward adds another weakness that comes from I-self isolationism. The I-self even gets isolated from his or her own body. "Listen to your body," my old Irish mother used to say. I-selves need that advice. The I-self egotist can easily act like a mind floating free, as though there were nothing else to us but that conscious mind. This can sever us from our rich store of feelings that well up from our unconscious. There are rich and helpful instincts in us, deeply rooted in our bodily feelings. I talked above about the ants and how their response to the common good is inscribed right into their genes. We are not so mechanically built, but we do have good instincts grounded in our genetic structure. We are born with gentle needs that foster society. In the final month of pregnancy, the little not-yet-born fetus is practicing smiling and sucking . . . both very sociable activities. Smiling takes a lot of facial muscular work, and the little creature is getting ready for it. When its eyes clear after birth, the baby smiles not at our elbows but at our faces. By genetic instinct it knows that the face, not the elbow, is the center of personality. We are all born with instincts to trust, to smile, to laugh, and to hug and be hugged. That's not a bad start. We start out as we-selves, thoroughly interwoven into the lives of others.

And there is more. We're not all bad. We are spontaneously geared to sensitivity in many ways. We have some naturally compassionate impulses. Harold Coward talks about the experience of swerving the car spontaneously to avoid hitting a dog. This is a somewhat dangerous thing to do, and if asked why you did it, you might reply that you simply reacted. It may be more complicated than that. Coward offers this interpretation: "At the first instant of seeing the dog, you spontaneously valued the dog and attempted to avoid harming it. Momentarily the dog was part of your extended we-Self." Had you had more time to think, a more selfish I-self might have calculated the risks and behaved differently—less compassionately. Similarly, upon seeing an accident, Coward says that there is a spontaneous impulse—as spontaneous as an infant's smile—to stop and help. It is easily overwhelmed by I-self concerns for one's own schedule, fear of a lawsuit, or thinking that somebody else will do it.

A lot of the world's religions attempt, through meditation, to heal this inner divorce between our conscious, calculating ego and our body-rooted instincts for compassion. We are capable of extending our affective response to the world, to all of it. We can move from a self-absorbed I-self to a well-related we-self. The world's religions work on this. Judaism, Christianity, and Islam all insist on extending our we-self potential to include all other humans. Asian and native religions actually go further. They extend it to include all animals, as well as organic and inorganic nature.

Coward says this effort of the aboriginal and Asian religions is potentially present in all of us. "We do seem to impulsively pull back from hurting animals, killing plants, or polluting earth, air, and water. But this momentary we-self impulse rapidly disappears under the stronger self-interest of the I-self." What is making the religions pay more attention to this now are the "challenges of overpopulation, unsustainable consumption, and the threatened destruction of the natural ecosystem itself."

In comparing I-self and we-self cultures, it would be a mistake to think that all these we-self cultures have been perfect in their treatment of the rest of nature. Just as Christians with their gospel of love have not always been loving, other religions have not always lived up to their best insights. Jesus urged Christians to nonviolence, telling them to turn the other cheek and love their enemies. You wouldn't know this from watching Catholic and Protestant Christians bombing and shooting one another in Northern Ireland for decades. This doesn't mean Christianity can't powerfully influence behavior for the good. Look how the Quakers struggled successfully for the liberation of women, the ending of slavery, prison reform, and the extension of education to all classes in society. Or look at Martin Luther King Jr.'s struggle to win human rights for African Americans. As the historian Garry Wills says, religion is a powerful social force. Most of the revolutionary movements that transformed, shaped, and reshaped the American nation, for example, "abolitionism, women's suffrage, the union movement, the civil rights movement . . . grew out of religious circles."

It helps to find examples of people living up to the best in their traditions. We see Native Americans with their religious view of nature carefully trying to leave nature as undamaged as they found it. We can find instances of other cultures and religions acting out the best that is in them. The fact that this doesn't always happen should not slow down our search for the best ideas and ideals available in the whole human family at this time of earth crisis. The challenge is to mine these traditions and take advantage of their treasures. Each of them is a storehouse of wisdom and practical advice. What Dr. Coward has done in this exercise is to emphasize a mindset, an outlook toward others and toward nature that can be a corrective to our self-centeredness. Our I-self approach can do with a bit of we-self thinking. Nature and other people would be better off for that. And we would be happier.

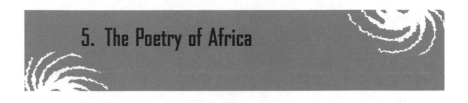

5. The Poetry of Africa

As WE LAUNCH INTO OUR TOUR OF WORLD RELIGIONS to see what they have to offer us and the planet we are busily wrecking, the obvious place to start is Africa. After all, we are all Africans. A few million years ago, evolution took some startling leaps in Africa, and the result is us. Four million years ago, our most distant ancestors, called hominids, appeared in what is now known as Tanzania and Ethiopia. The process issued forty thousand years ago into what we call Homo sapiens. This African ancestor ushered in the first signs of culture and civilization. Homo sapiens Africanus introduced complicated tools, harnessed the power of fire, planted the first crops, established the first village, spoke the first language, and engaged in both ritual and artistic activities. There was the beginning of humanity.

So what we have going for us began in Africa. Every human being either lives in Africa or is an emigrant from there. So let's go back home and taste the wisdom of our ancient homeland.

Before Christianity and Islam arrived in Africa, there were rich religious traditions regarding the naturalness of sharing and the need for reverence before the beauty of life. In the native African religions, land ultimately belonged to Ngai, the supreme god. In a way that parallels the Book of Leviticus in the Hebrew Bible, humans were seen as tenants only, and the earth was revered as a sacred trust. In the poetic rituals of ancient Africa, we, the animals, and the plants all share a common spiritual energy. A journey through the religious poetry of Africa could enrich all other religions. These religions are classics of reverence, and we should approach them as grateful students.

Our guide here will be Professor Jacob Olupona, a native of Nigeria, currently teaching at the University of California,

Davis. He taught for many years in Nigeria and still goes back there regularly. His special interest is in the native religions of Africa, religions that were formed before Christianity or Islam, though both of these religions have moved into Africa and commingled with the older African religions.

Before getting to the description of the religious treasures of Africa, Olupona invites us to take a look at contemporary Africa and to see the horrors wreaked upon it by the nations of Europe and North America. Western history books usually say something strange: they say that Africa was "discovered" by Portuguese explorers in the fifteenth century just as America was "discovered" by Columbus. The folks there didn't need to be discovered. They lived there. Discovery, of course, is the language of imperialism, and the discovery of Africa was a centuries-long story of rape and pillage. First on the rape list were the people, our blood relatives who trace back with us to the origins of humanity. Twenty million able-bodied men and women were kidnapped as slaves and taken to the Americas, where their descendants still suffer from racism and prejudice today. When the slave trade ended at the end of the nineteenth century, the colonial powers moved in and divided Africa into sections, much as organized crime divides cities and states into gang territories for exploitation.

The colonial powers crushed the gentler modes of sharing and living that had been built up in Africa over the centuries and proceeded to strip the land of every value and resource. The wealth of the Americas and of Europe is built to a substantial degree on this long-term plunder. In 1960, the nations of Africa began to free themselves of the colonial thieves, but things actually got worse. The exploiting nations had created small elites, braced with military power, and these natives began a new tyranny. In many places where a democracy had been established, military rulers, backed by foreign governments, unseated the democratic rulers and set up dictatorships. The joy of liberation in 1960 turned to bitterness. Most of Africa is worse off now than before independence. Rich elites coexisting with abject poverty stir resentment and violence.

There is general knowledge in the rest of the world that things are bad in Africa, and in a blame-the-victim way, most in the West feel that it must be the Africans' fault. As one African chief put it, they broke our legs and then they ask, Why can't you run, while others are running?

The ecology has been devastated by careless mining and resource extraction. Lake Victoria (notice the non-African name for this African treasure!), which had long been a source of life and nourishment for humans and animals alike, is polluted drastically. Poverty leads to chaos and disease. When Jacob Olupona taught in the Nigerian university, the community had to boil their water since they lacked money to buy chlorine to purify the local dam's water supply. Two of his students died one semester from typhoid fever, obviously caused by impure water. In some parts of Africa, one out of three persons is infected with the HIV virus. Imperialism, economic or military, is always a form of murder because the plunderers have little or no regard for the factors that enhance life for the natives.

It is not a pretty story, but Professor Olupona thought we should pause to look at it before looking at the vibrant religions of Africa. All of us who ignore the plight of Africa bear guilt. Admission of guilt is something that all the world's religions encourage. It cleanses the heart and opens the gateway to reform.

The Nature of African Religions

Africa is religiously complicated. There is no such thing as the one religion of Africa. Not only are there countless modes of native religions, but two large world religions entered Africa years ago, Christianity and Islam. These mixed in with the religions already there. In the north, Islam tended to be the main religious visitor; Christianity took more roots in the south of this great continent. Some interesting mixtures and hybrids formed as a result.

Our interest is in seeing the native religions of Africa so as to taste their special poetry and insight. Our chapter mentor, Professor Jacob Olupona, will lead us through some of the main myths and rituals that permeate African thinking and sensibilities. As in all chapters, we will be looking to see how these religious efforts addressed egoism, human rights, and just ownership; the status of the poor, of women, and of the rest of nature; and our right to a joyful life. We will be interested in how their insights and poetry might influence the huge problems of our earth, problems caused by overpopulation in many areas and overconsumption by the well-off.

First a word on myths, rituals, and symbols: Myths, especially other peoples' myths, seem strange—even weird. But myths are among the highest form of communication. Our Western culture is very verbal and rational and likes to get truth from tightly reasoned arguments and tidy graphs. Yet, in the history of all civilizations, the greatest insights are usually housed in symbols, myths, poetry, and rituals. They are loaded with psychology and social theory.

Take the Greek mythical figure Tantalus. He was invited by the gods to dine on Olympus. While there, he stole some ambrosia, the potion that gives the gods immortality. For his punishment, he was given immortality but made to suffer unending hunger and thirst. When he bends to the river to drink, it recedes from him, and when he reaches up for fruit, it rises beyond his grasp.

This is not seen by scholars as an idle little fairy tale, but as a symbol of the human desire to defeat death. There is a bit of Tantalus in all of us who expect medicine to keep us thrivingly well forever. It is just not possible. There is no ambrosia to save us from the diseases that eventually defeat all medicine. The insight of the myth is that it is wise to accept limits. We cannot defeat them all. The myth of Icarus is the same. He wanted to fly higher than humans should, to reach for impossible goals; his wings melted off and he crashed. Same message: there are limits.

So as we move into the ancient African myths, open your mind and imagination to the wisdom of people long since departed from earth life, people who wondered about the same things you and I do, people who have something to say to us.

For starters, African religions do not have a Bible. You can't find sacred texts that contain the gist of their vision as you can for Jews, Christians, and Muslims. What you do find is a rich store of myths and stories and rituals. Among their most interesting myths are what scholars call their cosmogonic myths, myths about how the world got started. First we turn to these myths of origin, and then we can see what we can take from them.

Among the Yoruba people, the story goes like this: Once upon a time, the sky god, Olorun, decided to create the world. He summoned a lesser god, Obatala, to do the job. Olorun did not send Obatala out empty-handed for this grand mission. He gave him a rooster, a package of soil, a chain, a chameleon, and a powerful magical object called the *ase,* which was a symbol of the very essence of the gods. The plot thickens. On the way to create the world, Obatala ran into a number of gods who were celebrating and drinking palm wine. He joined them and drank too much, got drunk, and fell asleep. Another god, Oduduwa, saw Obatala fast asleep and swiped all the materials for creation except the *ase.* He used the chain to descend to earth, poured the parcel of soil on the water, and placed the rooster on it. As this was done, dry land was created, vegetation formed along with animals. The chameleon was put on the earth to add to its variety.

When poor Obatala woke up, slightly hung over, he saw what had happened. He also saw that a lot of other gods, including the fiery god of war, had descended onto the earth to make mischief. Things were not going well. It was time for Olorun to step in. He summoned the two competing gods, Oduduwa and Obatala, back to his sky home and made a compromise. He let Oduduwa be the ruler over the world and its first sacred king, but he gave Obatala the job of fashioning human beings out of earth's soil. But notice this: in this arrangement, all the living forms of earth, plants, animals, and humans would be enlivened by the same *ase,* the divine energy.

These are the main lines of this myth, so what does it say? Like the myths of Tantalus and Icarus, it is loaded with messages. First of all—and this is very ecologically friendly—all plants and animals and humans share the same divine energy, *ase.* They are all sacred and all related. Kinship is very important in African cultures, and the plants and the animals are kin. They are family. This calls for enormous reverence for all that lives, even if tragically we must kill some of life to live ourselves—we live on plants, fish, and animals.

Like all peoples, the Africans use plants and herbs as medicine, but they were inclined to attribute the healing power not to the chemical makeup of the plant but to the common bond of kinship, of *ase* that bonds us to the rest of nature. Nature is basically our friend, though the confusion at the creation signals that it is not perfect.

There is another link with nature known as the totem. Totemism is another symbolic way of stressing the link between humans and the rest of nature. Many of the African societies held that certain people and certain clans had a kind of mystical (totemic) relationship with certain animals, plants, or trees. For example, Jacob Olupona is a twin, and his people held that twins are totemically related to the colobus monkey. There is a serious taboo against a twin killing or eating this animal. A number of poems celebrate the intimate relationship of this animal and all twins. Here is another link between humans and the rest of nature. In this relationship between human twins and these colobus monkeys, the violence that requires us to kill plants, fish, and animals to feed ourselves is suspended. The colobus monkey and the twins enjoy a nonviolent peaceful intimacy.

All the elements of this creation myth make the point that life is complicated and a little messed up right from the start. The primal arrangement was a deal struck with competing forces. The creation story is not all peaches and cream. It is not a paradise. Nasty forces like the god of war are afoot here, sowing violence. The whole story indicates that creation was not a perfect job—what with gods getting drunk and fighting with one another. The result was a compromise and not a perfect one. Our African ancestors were telling us that this is not a perfect world, but that life is a miracle, filled with divine energy. For all of its contradictions, life on earth is a wonder to be cherished. There is a strong tendency in these religions to blame us, not the gods, for the woes of earth. The myths have various ways of saying this.

The Africans believed in a three-tiered universe. The supreme being, thought of as either male or female, lived in the sky; we live in the middle section; and the ancestors live in the underground. In the original plan, some say, the sky was right next to earth, but the bad behavior of people caused the supreme god to move it way up out of our reach. The first humans set too many fires and the smoke drove God away to the distant sky. In other words, we are more of a problem than the squabbling gods who got the earth started. Environmental disasters offended this god and drove him or her to retreat from us. We are still closely related to the sky world. The rain and the lightning, the wind and the sun are all essential to our lives. The sky world is not an inaccessible and remote heaven. It is, rather, interacting with us day by day.

The earth and the precious topsoil on which all life depends is not a thing to be exploited and used carelessly. Rather, the earth is referred to as a living person, and the ground is this person's head. Tilling the soil is like combing a person's hair. Obviously, you should do it lovingly and tenderly, in a way that does not hurt.

The earth is also our destiny. We go there in death to join our ancestors. Death is described as bowing to the call of the earth. The idea of afterlife is not strong in these religions. There is no separate heaven to which we go after death. Ancestors, buried in the earth, live in our memory of them. Salvation also is something very this-worldly. The triple blessing followers of these religions pray for is sufficient wealth to live decently, healthy children, and a long and peaceful life.

Private Property

Every philosophy or religion contains a theory of ownership. The Romans, for example, came up with a theory of owning that has been bequeathed to much of the modern world, and it is a mess. It imagines the individual acquiring such an absolute right to own whatever he or she owns that the owner can use, profit from, or abuse it at will. All power goes to the owner. That which is owned, even if it is the land, can be used or abused by the owner. This toxic notion, which slipped like a virus into much of modern law, is ecologically and socially unfriendly. If you own the property, you can pollute it to death.

Not so in Africa. The African economy was an economy based on land for farming or grazing. Land, it was taught, belongs to the ancestors. The eldest in the clan had the right to use and protect the land, but it was a sacred trust, not an absolute right. It was a kind of communal ownership, and it certainly did not involve the right to abuse the land. The reverence that was felt for the ancestors was also felt for the land. This is a beautiful example of a we-self culture.

This gentle approach was trashed by the invading colonialists who brought in a kind of Roman-law notion of ownership. In British Kenya, for example, this was done with devastating results. First, the colonials seized the land and displaced the native people. Three thousand Britons took over land that was once gently cared for by four million natives. When the British left, the land passed over to the rich Kenyan elite, and the result was poverty and ecological destruction. The Mau Mau rebellion (1952–1954) was in response to this unjust situation, though most in the rest of the world dismissed it as some strange tribal war.

The same selfish notion of ownership was foisted on others as in South Africa, with similarly tragic results. The British and Dutch invaders acted like they were bringing civilization to these savages, whereas they were displacing lovely and gentle patterns of treating nature and the human community.

Rituals

The African rituals showed that they were in constant dialogue with the rest of nature. These rituals were again communal, with everyone taking part. If the land had been damaged, they went through ceremonies trying to find out what had spoiled the land. If it was found to be the fault of the community, a ceremony of cleansing the land, returning it to its original purity, was performed by all. Ritual grabs not just your mind but your emotions and imagination. The powerful rituals of giving thanks for bountiful harvests or cleansing the earth all pointed to the land as sacred gift and trust. Women often had a major part in these rituals, which showed their importance to the community and worked against male dominance. We could learn a lot from them.

Population Questions

As with most people throughout history, the African religions prized children highly and wanted more of them; they were the most sacred form of wealth. The people also tried to hold on to life as long as possible. Older people were revered, and it was a primary duty for children to care for them so that they could enjoy their old age.

The desire for more children is understandable in our species. Historically, depopulation was often the concern. Many ancient societies penalized bachelors and rewarded families for their fertility. Small wonder. These were societies where, as historian Peter Brown says, "death fell savagely on the young." Only four out of every hundred men—and fewer women—lived beyond their fiftieth birthday. As a species, we formed our populating habits in worlds that were, in Saint John Chrysostom's words, "grazed thin by death." Such instincts are deeply rooted. If, as the Jesuit paleontologist Teilhard de Chardin sagely says, nothing is intelligible outside its history, this reproductive thrust, especially in stressful conditions, is the defining story of our breed. It also affected the religions that were spawned in this kind of world.

Africa too reflects this love of large families. The desire for more children was part of the tendency toward polygamy in Africa. However, huge families are a problem in today's overcrowded world. The terrible massacres in Rwanda in recent years were related to the overpopulation and ecological spoiling of that area. What redemptive elements are there in African spirituality to cope with this?

First of all, according to Jacob Olupona, pregnancy was always seen as a family and community event, not a private little drama in life. Jacob was struck when Lady Diana of Britain observed that when she had her pregnancy of Prince William, she felt that the entire British nation was carrying the pregnancy with her. Says Olupona, "In African communities this is not just the privilege of the royals; the pregnancy of any village woman has special significance for the community." Thus there is a social dimension to pregnancy. That means that in an overcrowded community, the number of pregnancies should not exceed the resources of the community. This was realized in the various societies. Too many births can lead to too many deaths, they said. Births were not desired if the conditions for a peaceful and happy life were not there for the baby. Thus, there was openness to family planning, and this is being stressed anew in Africa.

What will also help with this problem is the African stress on frugality and sharing. They saw the division of a society into haves and have-nots as evil, and they had what Olupona sees as a natural immunity to "the global virus of consumerism." He tells how the Yoruba people call it a crime when there is "one rich person in a sea of two hundred poor people." The we-self was and is strong, and this can now be applied to judgments on population and overconsumption by the affluent. Africans are also beginning to see the futility and waste of spending money on useless military weapons that could be used to feed the hungry. Olupona tells the story of a schoolteacher in Nigeria in 1996 asking a student whether he had breakfast. The pupil's response was that it was not his turn that day to eat breakfast. There were six children in the family, and they had to take turns getting breakfast. These conditions clash with the call that fills African myths and rituals: respect for every person.

Visions from Africa

This trip into the religious stories of Africa does not tell us that Africa is perfect. Not at all. The sad fact of human life is that great ideals and visions can coexist with massive evils. African religion gives the basis for great respect of humans and all of nature, but this was not always lived any more than Christians always lived the gospel of love. Female genital mutilation is a widespread practice in Africa and is inexcusable. It is a horrid form of sexism. Modern Africans are now imitating the rest of us in savaging the earth. The only hope for the human race, however, is to first of all admit our sins and failings and then look for our better insights and saving dreams to try to save ourselves and our mother earth.

Africa has a vision for us. It has a deep sense of the common good, including the rest of nature, and not just us humans, in the definition of the common good. It places a high value on sharing, which is the very heart of justice. It gives high status to all people, whether poor, foreign, or female. All are animated with the same spirit. Their destiny is joy and celebration, not just grinding out a living. Africa in its religious traditions talks to us and says wise things.

We turn next to another wise neighbor in the human community, Buddhism.

6. Buddhism:
Lessons on Downsizing Wants

MUCH OF WESTERN CULTURE HAS NEVER LEARNED when enough is enough. We and our economics are driven by wants, not needs. Let me illustrate with a story. An American go-getter, hard-driving friend of mine was in Ireland trying to relax. An amateur painter, he was sketching scenes by the beach. He became fascinated and a little annoyed at an Irish lobster fisherman who arrived for his day's work around 10:00 A.M., paused on the dock for conversation, sipped a little tea at the shack, and finally pushed off around 11:00 or later. Back he came at around 2:30 in the afternoon with a few lobsters on board. Again, conversation on the dock, more tea, and then off to the market to sell his lobster catch.

Finally, my friend could not resist. He accosted the fisherman. Thinking that maybe the man fished so little because there were no fish there, he asked, "If you went out earlier and came back later, could you catch more lobsters?"

The man took his time answering because time was something he had lots of. After a while, he replied, "Oh yes, thank God, there's plenty of lobsters out there to be caught."

Then my calculating friend, wondering if the problem was market demand, asked, "If you caught more, could you sell them?"

"Oh, yes," he replied. "They love the lobsters and you can always sell them."

My friend, like a prosecuting attorney moving in for the kill, asked, "Then, why don't you do that?"

The fisherman, puzzled by the line of questioning, answered in all simplicity, "Enough is enough, you know."

But my friend did not know. He came from a culture built on enough never being enough.

The wisdom of Buddhism would be on the side of the Irish fisherman who had reached his own sort of nirvana. His needs were all met. He had time for conversation, laughter, and contemplation. He was not torn apart by unrealistic needs.

The world's religions are fascinating because they do more than talk about worship and the sacred. They also probe the inner core of human beings to see what makes us tick . . . and to show us better ways of ticking. They are all in-depth probes in psychology. Buddhism is a standout in this regard. Though every religion targets egoism with the zeal of radiologists going after cancer, Buddhism is relentless in showing how destructively self-centered and ravenously acquisitive the human animal is. Then it moves on to prescribe a cure.

Buddhism illustrates something that can be said about all the world's religions. As I have already said, they start out with simple yet profound insights, but as time passes, they take on a terrific overload of jargon and obfuscation to the point where their basic genius can be lost. In Christianity, for example, a lot of convoluted theology can obscure the simple but powerful moral message of the prophet Jesus.

In meeting Buddhism, our principal guide is Professor Rita Gross, a practicing American Buddhist. The Buddhist stress on simplicity in living was attractive to Gross partly in response to her early life. In her youth, she lived a simple life, close to nature, and far from the ravages of pollution. For eighteen years, she had no central heating, indoor plumbing, or processed foods. Her family lived without polluting pesticides and with no nearby neighbors. She writes: "Dragonflies, butterflies, fireflies, and many other beautiful creatures that I never see in my city lot abounded. Traffic noise was a novelty. At night one could see a million stars in the black sky." She still retreats at times to the old homestead, adding only a little electricity for lights and a computer. But things are different now. Her retreat is surrounded by houses packed together as though they were in a city. Cars and noise and dirt encroach, and light pollution whites out the nighttime sky once rich with stars. Dragonflies, butterflies, and fireflies are now something to comment on. There is almost no hiding from what we call modern life and its impact.

For Rita Gross, as hard as it is to do, living simply without overcrowding is the way into an "environmental paradise" for all. She thinks that it is possible to save this precious earth, and it is this vision and this hope that guides her presentation of the principal teachings of Buddhism. Though Buddhism began 2,500 years ago in a very different kind of world, the insights it had into the flaws and possibilities of human nature are still remarkably valid. Even though, historically, Buddhism was not applied to the problems of over-population and ecological destruction, the principles of Buddhism meet these problems head on.

There are, of course, many forms of Buddhism, but on many points almost all Buddhists agree. As with all religions, there is a kind of moral core that grounds everything else.

Here is a quick little catechism on Buddhism, with Rita Gross and other Buddhists as our guides.

The Four Noble Truths

Buddhism starts with the Four Noble Truths. The first truth is that conventional living produces unnecessary suffering. The second truth says that that suffering is produced by the ignorance and obsessive desires that conventional living engenders. To add a Sanskrit word to our vocabulary, the classical Buddhist word for this kind of desire is *trishna*. Buddhism is not out to eliminate desire. Indeed, the desire for harmony and wisdom is central to the tradition. But *trishna* is another thing entirely. It connotes insatiable demand and craving. It is *trishna* that explains the hyperconsumerism and the shop-'til-you-drop syndrome. The third truth draws the obvious conclusions that if you can be freed from these unrealistic and unsettling desires, you will be free from the suffering they produce. The fourth truth says that our freedom lies in living a life of wisdom, moral discipline, and spiritual depth. This last is the how-to truth.

The Ethics of Buddhism

The moral code of Buddhism, the how-to part, consists of five traditional precepts. Ancient Buddhists often considered these precepts or commandments as relating more to private life than to societal life with its politics and economics. Modern Buddhists, however, stress the application of the five precepts also to our full planetary plight. On to the five precepts.

1. The first is no killing, or no harming. This springs from the very heart of Buddhism, which is *compassion*. As the Dalai Lama says, Buddhism is essentially "a policy of kindness": kindness to other people, even enemies, and kindness to all of the rest of nature. At a time when we are witnessing the collapse of ecological systems and the poisoning of air, water, and food, the human race needs to be set onto a policy of kindness. The goal of the policy of kindness in this is that all of life should flourish. As Rita Gross says, "poverty has always been evaluated as spiritually useless by Buddhists." They don't preach a destructive asceticism. They see happiness and harmony as the marks of the good life, and all the precepts are pointed in that direction.

2. The second precept is not taking what is not given. That obviously matches the *Thou shalt not steal* of other moral traditions, but it states it in an interesting way. The target of this precept is greed. Apply this to our current ripping-off of poor countries with their resources so that we can live high on the hog. The global economy lures formerly self-sufficient farmers in the so-called third world into planting cash crops with the hope that they can be affluent but often leaves them in hunger and in debt. The global economy is built upon taking what is not given from poor nations and from the whole of nature, as wealthy nations gobble up renewable and nonrenewable resources. Greed has gone high tech and corporate. This is not a Buddhist way of life.

Buddhism has an answer to the question, What difference does it make? People might say, Why practice conservation in my little kitchen? or What difference does it make if I buy a smaller car or use my bicycle more often? Big-time corporate pollution dwarfs my little activities. The Buddhist answer is that your integrity matters. Living compassionately, not taking more than your share or dirtying the earth more than you must, means that you are living more truthfully, more honestly, less thievingly, and there is value in that.

3. The third precept is no lying. But in our world, lying too has been institutionalized. More money is spent on advertising than on higher education in the United States. And the purpose of advertising is not truth but profit and the creation of false need. Advertising is in the business of

trishna creation. It has to create a need in us for the latest upgrade of all our gadgets and toys. The crippling thing about this kind of obsessive desire, according to Professor Gross, is that the object of desire becomes more powerful, more in control, than the person who desires. *Trishna* doesn't let you stop and enjoy what you have. It sets you on a rat race of *wanting*. That is what the Buddha spotted as at the heart of much human suffering.

4. The fourth precept relates to sex and gender issues. It repudiates sex that causes pain to others. That is a healthy sexual maxim. Obviously, this rejects infidelity in a relationship because it can cause the unsuspecting partner the pain of betrayal and even disease. Many modern Buddhists apply this to gender relationships and support the full empowerment of women throughout society. Many also use it to support all healthy and responsible human relationships, including same-sex relationships. Buddhism feels that human happiness depends on achieving harmony even among those who are different from us. It doesn't specialize in bedroom ethics. It specializes in compassion and nonharming, and that has applications from bedroom to boardroom and beyond.

5. The fifth precept bans anything that clouds the mind. This was sometimes used to condemn all intoxicants, such as alcohol. Today it is also used to condemn the materialistic obsessive advertising that creates a never-enough mentality. It also would condemn the clouding of our minds that blinds us to the suffering in the world. Thus, it would indict news reporting that leaves most of the story untold or that reports only on what is of interest to the rich and the powerful, leaving out the stories of the poor. Buddhism is opposed to letting others impose on us a sense of reality. It wants us to take reality straight. It urges us to pause and meditate on what really is. In a sense, it says with the rappers, "Don't believe the hype!"

In the grips of *trishna,* you can't stop to revel in the good things that already are in your life. The mad rush to acquire gets in the way of enjoyment. The need for *more*—more prestige, more money, more gadgets, more upgrades—can be like the need of an alcoholic for more alcohol. Advertising seduces us and clouds the mind by turning luxuries into necessities, spawning insatiable hunger and discontent. The Buddhist teaching that enough is enough is a message that we feverish superconsumers need.

Buddhist Wisdom

The literature of Buddhism is immense, but we'll take a look here at three of its truly rich and special insights: interdependence, mindfulness, and compassion.

1. *Interdependence* is a major concept in Buddhism. As Rita Gross puts it: "Interdependence means that nothing stands alone apart from the matrix of all else." Everything we do sends ripples out that affect others, and "each of us feels the effects of actions taken far away by people whom we do not know." She continues: "Nothing that we do is irrelevant, without impact on the rest of our matrix." Going back to Harold Coward's terms, Buddhism presses us to think of ourselves as a we-self, not as an isolated and unrelated I-self. And the we of Buddhism does not just relate to people but to all that lives and exists upon the earth. Indeed, many Buddhists believe that at death we do not cease to exist but reemerge in another form of life. Whatever one may think of this idea of reincarnation, it does press home the relatedness of all things. Other religions such as Christianity and Islam believe in an afterlife, not one centered on this world but on an otherworldly heaven. In Buddhism, personal life is not segregated from the rest of nature by a destiny in a heaven.

How realistic is this ancient Buddhist concept of interdependence, with its belief that "nothing that we do is irrelevant, without impact on the rest of our matrix"? Actually, it is very congenial to modern science and to the facts of modern life. The modern ecology movement is stressing the impact of the rediscovery that we are in fact interconnected with all of nature. Science believes that all of life descended from a single cell. This seems to be the only way of explaining the basic similarity of all the cells of all living things on earth. All have the same DNA code and similar amino acids.

Life evolved into literally billions of species, but all forms of life seem to have the same common root. We are cousins to the flowers and the birds and even to the creeping things of the earth. Our proud isolation from the rest of nature—the nature on which we totally depend anyhow—is unrealistic. It allows us to proceed with the wrecking of life on earth with our lavish lifestyles. Buddhism and science together remind us that we are all part of the same primeval miracle whereby life started on this earth.

By meditating, Buddhists try to deepen their sense of relatedness to all that is. It's an energizing experience and a kind of reality therapy. A sense of our real connectedness is good for our spirits.

Thinking of ourselves as separate, independent beings is an illusion that feeds our frenzied cravings. That independent self, in fact, does not exist. It is a nonself—*anatman,* the Buddhist calls it. But, Professor Gross continues, that *"anatman* is simply another name for interdependence."* The fiction that we are a self-existing, self-contained bundle of wants and needs whose existence ends with our skins is dangerously unreal and unfriendly to all our biological neighbors. It is the very root of egoism, and egoism is the original sin of our species. To be is to be *with* and *of* all others.

This does not mean that all living things are of equal value. People are more precious than nasty viruses, and so are birds and peonies and puppy dogs. But we are all part of the same grand and mysterious phenomenon called life. Everything that lives is related, and we should treat all that lives with respect and with a powerful sense of oneness—all of nature, the birds and trees, and the other innocent victims of our human-polluted air and water.

2. *Mindfulness.* Buddhism is convinced that we are never fully aware of the good things that we have or the evil we are doing. Buddhism targets ignorance and delusion. We cannot even appreciate what we have, so distracted are we by the quest for more. The Buddhist teacher Thich Nhat Hanh observes that we cannot even take time to appreciate "with calm awareness" the cup of tea we are drinking. We gulp it down, distracted by wandering thoughts, music, or noisy

conversation. This is, he insists, a form of violence. We do violence to the tea, to ourselves, and to the moment—a moment that will never be back. We are rushing into the future, hardly noticing the present. This would apply to other things we do, including making love; being with friends; enjoying music, art, an idea, or a garden.

Buddhism wants us not to become blasé but to look for the glory of the commonplace. The story is told of two men laying bricks. One man was asked what he was doing, and he replied curtly, "Laying bricks." The second man replied with delight, "I'm building a cathedral!" They were both building a cathedral, but one was caught in the drudgery of it. The eyes of the first man were lowered, and perspective was lost. He was not *mindful.* All our duties—from raising children to going to work—always have greater long-term meaning. Bowed heads don't see the horizons. We often lose sight of the cathedrals we are building.

When we are not mindful of the miracle that people are and nature is, we do harm. Pause for a moment of mindfulness on something all of life depends on, something that we are wasting by the ton on a daily basis. I speak of topsoil, that resource that is more precious than gold. We are *unmindful* of what it is. Author Annie Dillard tells what biologists find in a single square foot of topsoil one inch deep. It contains some 1,356 living creatures, including 865 mites, 265 springtails, 22 millipedes, 19 adult beetles, and various numbers of 12 other forms plus 2 billion bacteria and millions of fungi, protozoans, algae, and innumerable other creatures that make the topsoil the life-producing miracle it is. And yet, we waste it shamefully, *mindlessly.* By not protecting it in farming, we let it blow away. Scientist David Pimentel reports that measuring stations pick up Chinese soil in Hawaii when plowing season opens in China, and African soils blow in the wind in Florida when they start to plow. There are ways of protecting this soil, but we are not *mindful* or caring enough to use them. This is all the more tragic since, given our mental equipment, we could be the most mindful of animals. How the rest of nature wishes we were!

Buddhists also call our attention to the dangers of unmindful sex. Most Buddhists have very positive and joyful views of sex and Buddhism, and they discourage fear and needless guilt about sexuality. Buddhism urges a "mindful sexuality, involving the use of birth control unless appropriate and responsible pregnancy is intended," in Professor Gross's words. She says that excessive reproduction is a form of greed.

3. *Compassion.* The Dalai Lama sums up his religion simply. "This is my simple religion. There is no need for complicated philosophies, not even for temples. Our own brain, our own heart is our temple. The philosophy is kindness." He calls the practice of Buddhism a "policy of kindness." This kindness is not just smiling and beaming at people. It looks to the cruel structures and systems of economics and politics and searches for ways of living that are kinder to people and to nature. Helena Norberg-Hodge, an expert on economics, Buddhism, and ecology, points out the gentler systems being pioneered on earth to save people from the effects of an unfeeling global capitalism. She writes of the pioneering revival of local bartering that is replacing dependence on both money and distant global powers. There are plans known as Local Exchange and Trading Systems sprouting in England, Ireland, Canada, France, Argentina, Australia, New Zealand, and the United States. The systems arrange for the bartering of a wide range of services: carpentry, car repair, baby-sitting, sewing, teaching school, house painting, accounting, health care, legal assistance, as well as exchanging locally grown farm products and locally manufactured goods. Without money intervening, people barter what they can do for what they need—baby-sitting for carpentry or legal help, etc. As a result, a large number of people who were unemployed, and therefore deemed useless by the capitalistic system, are suddenly valued for their skills. That is a policy of kindness in action.

Another ongoing experiment is the Community Supported Agriculture (CSA) movement. In this system, consumers link up directly with farmers nearby. In some cases, consumers purchase an entire season's needed produce in advance, thus sharing the risk with the farmer. Consumers can visit the farms and even help out. This is allowing small-scale farmers to succeed. CSAs have been spreading in Europe, the United States, Australia, and Japan. Farmers' markets are another manifestation of local independence. This makes so much sense. As David Pimentel says, a head of iceberg lettuce is 95 percent water and contains just fifty calories of energy. It takes four hundred calories of energy to grow that head and another 1,800 to ship it. The lettuce has almost no nutrition. "Cabbage is better," says Pimentel, "and we can grow it in upstate New York." And elsewhere. This is localization as opposed to globalization, and it is kinder to people and to nature.

A final note on Buddhism. You don't have to convert to Buddhism. You can tap its wisdom and use its practices to increase your liberation and spirit of generosity without dis-affiliating from the religion you now practice. As in all these chapters, I have only scratched the surface of this religion. Further readings are suggested at the end of this book.

7. Hinduism's Rivers of Wisdom

IT CAN BE SAID OF ALL THE WORLD'S GREAT RELIGIONS that they are revolutions that got sidetracked. The challenge today is to try to get back to their original dynamism and apply it to our half-wrecked world. Hinduism, like the other religions, got seduced by lesser visions. As Hindu scholar Vasudha Narayanan says of Hindu India, "India is on the fast track to repeat the mistakes of the West." Narayanan will be our principal tour guide as we travel to India to bathe in the rivers of wisdom that flowed in the best of Hinduism. She is a native of India who now teaches at the University of Florida.

Hinduism is a product of India, and that signals that getting a handle on it is not going to be easy. India is a complex and varied land. In the United States, there is a lot of controversy about admitting Spanish as a second American language in certain contexts. India must smile at that. There are sixteen official languages in India and myriad unofficial ones. And out of all that disunity, India has managed to build a working democracy. Out of that also, it has produced the religion that we call Hinduism. Some say that Hinduism is not so much a religion as a confederation of varied religions. Some scholars almost despair of defining Hinduism, saying that Hinduism is simply the remainder that is left over in South Asia when you subtract all the other religions that exist there, including those of Muslims, Jains, Buddhists, Christians, and Jews. But that is too pessimistic. There are themes and practices and outlooks that are at home in the hearts of almost all Hindus, and Professor Narayanan and other scholars can share them with us.

Caricature Assassination

Robert McAfee Brown, a great Christian theologian, said that when visiting another religion, the first task is caricature assassination. Admit that our knowledge of other religions is fouled by many caricatures of what they are. When you approach a serious look at Hinduism for the first time, you probably do not do so expecting powerful lessons about the seductions of materialism, insights on ownership and its relationship to the common good, and dramatic rituals respecting nature and incorporating the wonders of nature into the heart of worship. We are more likely to know the downside. And downsides there always are. Christians have to live with the memory of the Inquisition and the bloody Crusades and the participation by many Christians in the Holocaust of World War II. Hindu India also has its horrors.

There is, for example, the terrible practice of *sati,* widow burning. The story of Roop Kanwar, an eighteen-year-old woman, was heard around the world. On September 4, 1987, she sat upright on the logs of her husband's funeral pyre and burned to death. She was a tragic example of an ancient Indian custom that is with us still in spite of efforts by India to stamp out this brutality that is sanctioned by no Hindu texts. There are, however, ancient Hindu texts that are thoroughly sexist as when the Hindu lawgiver Manu says, "In childhood a female must be subject to her father, in youth to her husband, when her lord is dead to her sons; a woman must never be independent." Bad ideas do not just stay in texts; they explode into real life. The hatred of women appears in the custom of the dowry. As modern consumerist poisons infect India, the dowry has become a source of terror. Aside from the original dowry, the in-laws demand continual payments, and when the woman cannot produce enough, she may be murdered, often by burning. At least two women are killed this way in New Delhi alone every day. The caste system also is ugly and unworthy of any modern state or major religion. With all of this in India, why would we repair there in search of wisdom and moral uplift?

Ghandi as Hindu Hero

Sometimes a single word can answer a question. To the question I have just asked, the word is Gandhi. Here was one of the moral heroes of our time, perhaps *the* outstanding hero of our age, and he was every bit the Hindu. He was fully aware of the evils that had grown up around him, but he searched into the deep wells of Hindu spirituality and fought the badness that came to India from within and from without. More than anyone in modern times, he showed the practical power of nonviolence to a world in love with kill-power, and he championed the value of economic empowerment in small and local ways. Gandhi said that "no person could be actively nonviolent and not rise against social injustice no matter where it occurred." He defended the cruelly treated Untouchables of India, the people who were condemned to clean public toilets. He cleaned the toilets with them and invited respectable Indians to do the same. He imposed no burden on his followers that he would not bear. As a result, even people who lost money due to boycotts he organized supported him gladly. Small wonder that he inspired other moral heroes, like Martin Luther King Jr. Gandhi could also use wit in his teaching. When asked once what he thought of Western civilization, he replied, "I think it would be a good idea!" He also said humankind thought its main challenge was to remake the earth, but that was wrong. Gandhi said it is remaking ourselves that is the real and crucial challenge.

In the twentieth century, when technical genius and horror both reached new peaks, Gandhi was a beacon of hope. This man who weighed less than a hundred pounds and whose net worth at his death was less than two dollars, was the hero of modern spirituality. He was also the hero of Hinduism and proof that this religion has something to teach us.

Gandhi had a hospitable mind that was open to inspiration from any source. He reached into the Christian Gospels and elsewhere looking for wisdom because, like a true Hindu, he did not believe that any religion has a monopoly on the truth. Many Hindus will concede that Jesus is an incarnation of God and that the Buddha was too; they feel that incarnations are a regular event, scheduled by God on the basis of need. As one Hindu put it, God seems to find recreation in variety, so there is good in all religions, and all worldviews deserve a hearing.

All of the great religions of the world are probes into what makes humans tick. Though not dressed up in the language of modern psychology, they are classical studies of human motivation. Five hundred years before Jesus walked among us, the Hindu epic *Mahabharata* gave a graphic and prophetic portrayal of what humans could do to the earth. It predicted huge population increases and ecological disaster. The trees would not bear fruit; drought would prevail; people would destroy parks and trees; and ruination would visit all of nature. This was not a magical power to predict the future. This was an insight into human nature, a wise and realistic estimate of the destructiveness of our species. Of course, at the time the epic was written, we did not have the technical capacity to be effective earth wreckers, but the authors saw that we had it in us.

Hinduism is also realistic about our wants and needs. It doesn't pretend that we were made to be austere ascetics, even though it admires the discipline of ascetics. It acknowledges that everyone seeks *artha* (Sanskrit for "affluence" and "power" and "recognition") and that we naturally look for *kama* (sensual pleasure). That's the way we are, and Hinduism insists we face up to these facts of life. The people of India also recognize that education does not just come from staring at words or reading analysis charts. It surprises many Westerners that Hindu teachers often turn first to art, dance, and ritual to teach. People may learn more from dance and drama than from written pages.

Ahimsa

The sages of India, however, knew that our cravings for sensual and power fulfillment could destroy us and the earth if not directed morally, and so a rich ethics was constructed. The cornerstone of this ethics was the belief that the entire universe is pervaded by the divine under various names. The world was in effect seen as the body of God. As a result, the prime moral obligation was one they call *ahimsa*, another Sanskrit word for our growing vocabulary. *Ahimsa* is usually translated as "nonviolence," as not doing any harm to any creature or to creation. An ancient text puts it this way:

> Knowing that the whole universe, whether animate or inanimate, is pervaded by the spirit of Rama, I ever

adore the feet of all with folded hands. Eight million
four hundred thousand species of living beings, classified under four broad divisions, inhabit land, water, and
the air. Realizing the whole world to be pervaded by
Sita and Rama, I make obeisance with folded hands.

Ahimsa was the heart of Gandhi's spirituality. His life
involved a struggle with the British domination of India, but
he would never permit his followers to think of the British as
evil. He said they must be thought of as brothers and sisters
of the Indian people. The goal of ahimsa is to change our
hearts from hostility to peace and to do the same for our
oppressors. The system of British oppression had to be
fought without hating British people. This was precisely the
main lesson that Martin Luther King Jr. took from Gandhi.
Enmity must be conquered by respect. Otherwise, hatred
reproduces itself, and the result is sheer hell. As Katherine
Young, a noted Hindu scholar, writes: "Far from seeing the
British as moral cretins, Gandhi respected them as people
with moral sensibilities that would eventually support Indian
independence. And he was correct."

A frequent theme in Hindu scriptures is this: "Nonmalice
to all beings in thought, word, and deed; compassion and
giving; these are the eternal dharma (duty) of the good."
And, the Hindus insist: this works, and violence ultimately
does not.

Hindu thinkers like Vasudha Narayanan are applying
Hindu teaching on ahimsa to population issues. Obviously,
when population exceeds carrying capacity, the results are
violent. Resources are finite, not infinite, and when there are
too many of us, we can ask for more than the earth has to
give. At that point, procreation can be an act of violence.

India has population problems. There is much in Hinduism, as in most world religions, that encourages fertility.
Small wonder. Staying alive in India was a challenge. As
recently as 1947, life expectancy was only thirty-two years. It
is now up to sixty-two years. This declining mortality is one
cause of the population surge that may soon make India the
largest population in the world—larger even than China.
Hunger is rising with the numbers of people. The average

consumption of grain in Canada is 974 kg per person per year; in the United States, it is 860 kg. In India it is 180 kg, and this is verging on starvation levels. Obesity is not a problem for India's poor.

Narayanan and others are addressing this. She points out that the problem is not just numbers but maldistribution. Food sharing was a matter of dharma and was religiously encouraged. The British, with their stress on individualistic independence and the work ethic, discouraged this sharing. Narayanan stresses the need for family planning, for the availability of contraception, and for abortion as a backup option. However, her main stress is on the empowerment of women. Education is the best contraceptive. Women who are educated are more likely to manage their fertility. Providing microloans to enable women to have financial independence is also effective in fertility management. The economic empowerment of women is a sure step toward sensible family planning.

India provides a sterling example of how the education of women can affect birthrates. Although the overall fertility rate in India is 3.4 children—replacement level for a stable population is thought to be 2.1 children—the Indian state of Kerala is a stunning success story. With a poverty rate worse than the average in India, Kerala's fertility rate is 1.8, and its fertility rate is falling faster than the fertility rate in the United States. The life expectancy for a Keralite male is seventy, while that of a North American male is seventy-two. The typical marrying age in Kerala is twenty-two as opposed to eighteen in the rest of India. The life expectancy of women in Kerala exceeds that of men, just as in the affluent world.

This is credited to the powerful tradition of participatory democracy in Kerala nourished by literacy—Kerala is less caste-ridden than any other part of the Hindu world—and especially by the strong and long-term commitment to women's education. Female literacy is at 87 percent compared to 68 percent in China. The dropout rate for girls from grades one to five is an almost unbelievable 0 *percent,* and some districts of Kerala have recently celebrated 100 percent literacy.

At this point, you could say that with Hinduism's stress on gentleness and nonviolence, it is a pity that India is not more Hindu. India is not a portrait of "nonmalice to all beings." The rivers of India are turning into cesspools, and its good soil and vegetation are being poisoned. Knowing the centrality of water to all of life on earth . . . knowing that we and the rest of nature are alive only because we are the one and only water planet, Hindus called their rivers sacred, poetically describing them as gods. But as Vasudha Narayanan says, "The ecologically insensitive values of market capitalism have reached our rivers; competing definitions of the sacred have undone gentler Hindu valuations."

But before we point fingers at the Indians and charge them with infidelity, we have to confess that just as India is not Hindu enough, so too Christian lands are not Christian enough; Muslim are not Islamic enough; and modern Israel is not Jewish enough. That is the human problem. It is what makes us a dangerous species. We can come up with gentle ideas such as *ahimsa,* but our greed prevails. *Ahimsa* versus violence is the main plot for the central planetary drama, and we are all players. Life on the planet is good or bad depending on whether *ahimsa* or violence prevails.

Dharma

Tied to *ahimsa* is another basic Hindu concept that goes by the name of dharma. *Dharma* is often translated as "justice" or "moral duty." The earth and all its residents are precious; indeed, they are the very body of the gods in Hindu thinking and should be treated accordingly. Scholars can debate whether Hinduism is ultimately monotheistic, believing in the oneness of God, or polytheistic. However that debate goes, the Hindus have a firm sense that reality is pervaded by sacredness. One of their names for divinity (Vishnu) means all pervasive. The bottom line is that the proper response to this marvel of a universe is reverence and gratitude, whether that gratitude is due to one god or multiple gods or just to reality. Thanksgiving, gratitude for the gift of being, as Narayanan says, "is the eternal dharma," the eternal duty. *You can't abuse that for which you are truly grateful.* That's a truth that fits in every faith and every ethic.

Dharma, then, is doing justice to people and to the earth. Dharma is what makes you holy. It unites you with the divine power that pervades the universe. Dharma is our duty. Duty, however, can have a grim and annoying sound to it. Not so, say the Hindus. Dharma is good for you. If people are just to one another, if they practice dharma, life will be sweet. If we practice dharma toward the rest of nature, it will be better for us. The Hindu Laws of Manu (an ancient set of laws that may or may not really be traceable to Manu) say that observing and protecting dharma protects us. Hindu leaders apply this to ecology and see tree planting as a kind of holy communion. Hindu temples say that tree planting is divine work and incorporate it into the worship. Signs on billboards proclaim: "A tree when protected protects us." One initiative counts 2.5 million trees planted. Some women have started what they call a Hugging Trees movement, again connecting piety and ecology. Efforts to clean up the rivers is also seen as religious duty. Divine grace is said to rush through your body as you clean up and nourish the suffering earth or respond to the needs of the Untouchables who exist in every society.

Karma

Karma basically means "work," but it has much more meaning tucked into it. It means that our every action or thought leaves traces on our character. As Professor Huston Smith, a historian of world religions, puts it: "Each thought and deed delivers an unseen chisel blow that sculpts one's destiny." Karma carries the strong Hindu conviction that our lives are what we make of them. They downplay the common Western idea that life is ruled by Lady Luck. Karma thinking says that whether we are happy or not is our doing. We get what we deserve.

Apply this to our social conscience. It is not bad luck that air, water, and soil are poisoned. That poison is our karma achievement. If our local or national government is bad, that's not just bad luck. It is to some degree the product of our indifference and that of the masses of people who don't bother to vote. If corporations rule the world, increasing poverty at the base of society and polluting the planet, it's because we all have let them do so. The idea of karma is hard-nosed. It says, Stop whining. You sowed, and you are reaping.

There is another side to karma. As we noted in discussing Buddhism, what we as individuals do seems of little moment. What difference does it make if we tilt toward a vegetarian diet to slow down the waste of grain protein on animals? Fast-food hamburgers are being pumped out by the billions anyhow. What good does our little gesture do if we bicycle rather than burn fossil fuel, wash our clothes with cold water, or restrain our use of air conditioning and heating to lower our energy use? So what? Everyone else on the block is riding in a sports utility vehicle and overheating their homes.

The doctrine of karma challenges this rationalization. It asks us, Do you put so little value on yourself? Everything you do makes you more or less selfish, more or less close to the divine. All major religions are obsessed with our egoism, the cardinal sin on which all human evil hinges. Each act that you perform and thought that you think makes you more or less self-centered, more generous or more mean-spirited. That mysterious *self* that peeks out through your eyeballs is in a constant process of formation. The traces of your behavior are the karma that makes you.

Many Hindus entertain the idea common in Asian religions that we do not die at death but are reborn in another form. Our karma rules our destiny and determines whether we can escape from this constant rebirthing and achieve the rest of nirvana. Whatever one makes of this mythology, it houses a lesson on responsibility. It says, Your actions count, and not even the slightest of them is meaningless. The flutter of a butterfly's wings has an impact on the universe, we are told. Our flutterings are no less significant.

The Meditative Pause
Hinduism, like other religions, especially those in the East, urges us to step out of the rat race that life can become and, in Gandhi's words, "shine the light within." In other words, take a meditative look at yourself, and see what you have become. Just as Christianity believes that you must be "born again of the Holy Spirit," Hindu teachers were convinced

that we drift into a way of thinking and living that is totally inauthentic. We need a total change of mind to see how much we have shortchanged ourselves and underestimated our possibilities. The practice of yoga involves many methods of helping us to rethink who we really can be. Certain stories were told also in Hinduism to illustrate this need for psychological and moral rebirth. One of the more interesting ones is the one about the tiger cub. Here is the story:

Once a pregnant tigress was ravenously hungry. After days of searching, she came upon a herd of wild goats. She leaped hungrily after one of them, missed, and the violence of the spring brought on the birth throes. Weak and exhausted, she gave birth and died. The little cub clung to her helplessly. The goats who had scattered returned to graze and found the poor creature, whimpering beside its dead mother. They took pity on it, suckled it with their own offspring, and cared for it fondly. The cub grew, learned their gentle way of bleating, and, with some difficulty, managed to survive on their diet of grass. One night, after some months, the herd was attacked by another tiger. The goats fled, but the cub stayed there without fear. He was, of course, amazed at the appearance of this huge beast. He bleated self-consciously and bent down to chew on the grass.

The old tiger roared in disgusted amazement. "What are you doing there, chewing that stuff and making those silly sounds?" He then seized the terrified cub by the scruff of the neck, dragged him to a pond, and made him look at their reflected visages. The cub was startled at how similar he was to the grand tiger, but there was more. The tiger dragged him to his den and insisted he eat some meat that lay there on the ground. The poor cub shuddered with disgust. The jungle tiger ignored his weak bleat of a protest and forced him to chew it and swallow. The cub's teeth were not ready for the meat, but he kept at it out of fear.

Suddenly he caught the full flavor of the blood and the exhilarating effect of the meat entering his body. He felt himself coming alive with a strange new strength. His whole body seemed to glow with a new energy. He smacked his glistening lips, opened his mouth, and for the first time in his life, let out the bellowing mighty roar of a tiger. The old tiger nodded and said: "Now, at last, you know who you are."

This story, or parable, which sounds like something that would be on a children's show, has a profound message. Actually, the message is like the one that Judaism and Christianity teach when they talk of the kingdom of God. That kingdom is what the world would be like if we were filled with the compassion of God for all that lives. In a word, we underestimate ourselves. We underestimate what the world could be. We underestimate our imaginations and the improvements we could make in our relationships. We waste money on military spending that could be used for schools, for the purification of water, for the saving of topsoil, and for ending poverty for all the children and people of this earth. We live in ways that destroy our environment, and we end up choking on our own poisons. We're tigers, and we live like goats. (It's not for us to change the Hindu myth, but it might have been better to have a goat hero, since goats live simpler and gentler lives.) A main point of the myth is that we need a teacher, like the grand tiger, to take us by the scruff of our necks and show us what a world marked by *ahimsa* could be. We need to be taught to think big and to think gentle. The rest of humankind and the planet itself await the blessing that could be.

8. Ancient Chinese Secrets

CHINA SOMEHOW MANAGED TO EXPORT MORE OF ITS KITCHEN than its culture. We all know what Chinese food is, and we are beginning to hear more and more about Chinese acupuncture. Interestingly, both are clues as to what Chinese culture is—and also as to what Chinese religion is—because religion is a major force in the makeup of culture.

If there is one word that has primacy in Chinese wisdom and culture, that word is *balance*. *Harmony* would be a companion term. This shows up in their cuisine. As Daniel Overmeyer, an expert on Chinese culture, says, "The typical Chinese dish does not consist of chunks of meat and vegetables on separate plates, but small pieces of several ingredients, each contributing to a harmonious taste." There it is. From the Chinese viewpoint, life, and indeed the universe, is seen as basically a harmonious whole. We are all interrelated and interdependent little parts of this mysterious heaven and earth where we find ourselves as privileged residents. The role of morality and of religion is to realize and enhance that harmony. The Chinese meal is successful if it balances the bitter and the sweet, the peppery and the bland, and multiple meats or fish. Their meal, like life, is a balancing act.

I spent a year as a guest professor at the University of Notre Dame. There were several Chinese graduate students in engineering living in the same residence hall. These were very busy young men, acquiring doctorates in science and doing it all in a foreign language. Time was precious for them. And yet, every evening, they came together to prepare supper together. It was the social event of the day, marked by conversation and laughter. Other American graduate students would rush over to the cafeteria and have a quick supper, often alone. Not the Chinese. They spent more than an hour every day just in the preparation of the diverse foods. They became, like the meal, a harmonious community.

In the morning, I would see them out doing those slow and graceful exercises most of us have seen on television. They are known as *tai chi*. Some of the movements of tai chi were originally imitations of animals, our companions on earth. In tai chi, the energy of the universe is invited to flow through the bodies of the dancers—and it is more dance than plain old exercise! This movement tends to be done in meditative silence, but, as ever, in a group. I found myself in awe of the Chinese students' sense of community and their reverence for life.

So now let's depart on a little tour of this ancient and wise culture. Our guide for this visit is Professor Chun-fang Yu, a gentle native of China who returns there frequently to do research on Chinese religion and culture. Professor Yu is distressed by the mess we are making of this lovely planet. She notes the realism of the formula used by environmentalists: *population x consumption x technology = environmental impact.* The more of us there are, the more we consume, and the more we develop technology, the more the earth groans under our weight. When more and more of us are consuming more and more, we start running out of resources, and we start overtaxing the earth's "sink capacity," as it is called, or garbage disposal capacity.

Yu points out that "the classic religions of the world have never faced a challenge like this. Since most of the world religions, including the Chinese religions, appeared long before the population explosion, excessive consumption, and ecological degradation became problems, it is obvious that we will not find specific teachings on these topics." Nonetheless, she believes that "a fundamental reexamination of our values and beliefs is essential before we can change our lifestyles and ways of thinking" so that we might develop a "loving instead of an injurious relationship with the earth and our fellow inhabitants both human and nonhuman." It is in that spirit that she leads us on a tour of Chinese religions.

There are three main religions in Chinese history: Confucianism, Taoism, and Buddhism. Yu is not interested on this tour in going into the history and differences of these three religions. That would make sense in a class on world religions. What she will lead us to is their common ground, those ideas and ideals that "met with approval among all Chinese people" and could help us form a new vision of the earth.

A Very Different Worldview

Before reading about some of the Chinese ideas on the meaning of reality, it does us Westerners good to remember how sophisticated the ancient Chinese people were, even scientifically. The Chinese made the first seismograph when Jesus was still alive and were systematically charting spots on the sun a generation before Jesus was born. People like this deserve a hearing, especially since Western culture has been too long deprived of Eastern wisdom.

Now on to their religion. When we in the Western world think of religion, we think mainly of Judaism, Christianity, and Islam. These religions are theistic to the core; that is, they all believe in a personal god. It is even hard for persons in the West to think of religion in any other way. If, however, we want to be open to other cultures and their wisdom, we must try to open our nervous eyes and see the different conclusions drawn by other good people trying to make sense of the universe. As Professor Yu tells us, "Unlike most other religions, Chinese religion does not have a creator god. There is no god transcendent and separate from the world, and there is no heaven outside of the universe to which human beings would want to go for refuge." That's a shocker to most people in our part of the world, but let's see where this kind of thinking led the Chinese. Unlike the Jewish Scriptures that start their origins story with "In the beginning . . . ," there is no beginning of the universe for the Chinese. It always was.

What there is is the universe, "heaven and earth," as they say, and that, Yu tells us, "is the origin of everything including human beings." There is in the universe a creating and sustaining force—the tao—pointing toward harmony, and conforming to that is our moral duty. Everything in the universe, from people to plants to rocks, is made of the same stuff, called *ch'i*. Since we are all so different, we and the rocks and the plants and the animals, how can we be made of the same stuff? The answer was that the differences come from variations in density, clarity, and form.

This may seem strange, but it is actually very close to modern science, which tells us that no clear line exists between life and nonlife. As Larry Rasmussen says in his monumental book *Earth Community, Earth Ethics,* "all of us, all creatures past, present, and future, began in stardust and evolved in the transformations of the universe on its long pilgrimage to date." To adapt the Catholic Ash Wednesday mantra, stardust we are and unto stardust we shall return. The Chinese were on to something like this millennia before the advent of modern science.

Yin and Yang

Reality, they also noted, is full of polarities such as day and night, bitter and sweet, winter and summer, male and female. They called this *yin* and *yang,* and this is why everything, including a meal, should be in conformity with this, balancing the bitter and the sweet, the peppery and the bland. This reality of which we are born, with its yin and its yang, with everything and everybody made of the exact same material, that is, *ch'i,* deserves our fullest respect. One word for that respect was *jen,* the greatest of the virtues as far as Confucius was concerned. *Jen* implies a largeness of heart, sincerity, compassion. It is the very essence of true humanity. To have it is to be a truly humane person. If you had *jen,* national boundaries would mean nothing to you because humanity is a shared glory. We are all made of the same basic stuff. Damaging nature would make no sense. We are all part of the same miracle. You can see where it led many Chinese to become vegetarians, since they would desire to do as little killing as possible to stay alive.

This comes close to the wisdom of Native Americans. Chief Seattle of the Squamish tribe wrote to the president of the United States in 1854: "Teach your children what we have taught our children: that the earth is their mother. Whatever befalls the earth befalls the children of the earth. . . . The earth does not belong to us; we belong to the earth." The Chinese agree. We are children of heaven and earth, and we should revere our mother.

All of this can be seen in the "Inscription" that is seen as a Confucian creed. It goes like this:

> Heaven is my father and Earth is my mother, and even such a small creature as I find an intimate place in their midst. Therefore that which fills the universe I regard as my body, and that which directs the universe I consider as my nature. All people are my brothers and sisters, and all things are my companions. The great ruler (the emperor) is the eldest son of my parents (Heaven and Earth), and the great ministers are his stewards. Respect the ages—that is the way to treat them. Show deep love toward the orphaned and the weak—this is the way to treat them. The sage identifies his character with that of Heaven and Earth. Even those who are tired, infirm, cripples, or sick; those who have no brothers or children, wives or husbands, are all my brothers and sisters who are in distress and have no one to turn to. In life I honor and serve Heaven and Earth. In death I will be at peace.

Suddenly, in that list of virtues, Jews, Christians, and Muslims will hear the voice of Isaiah, Jesus, and the prophet Muhammad urging us to have compassion on the orphans and the widows and to make the cause of the poor our cause. This we must do, the Chinese say. It is "the Mandate of Heaven," a powerful concept in Chinese morality and politics. Notice in the Confucian creed just given above where the emperor fits in. He is a brother born of the same parents, heaven and earth. He also must obey the Mandate of Heaven, that is, the moral law, and when he does not do that, the rascal can be thrown out, dethroned, and replaced by someone more filled with compassionate *jen*—someone more attuned to the mandate.

Reality is not capricious in this Chinese view. There is a law of nature, the Mandate of Heaven, and there is trouble if it is violated. No one, including the emperor, is above it. There was no divine right of kings in this doctrine, because the mandate was above the king and the people could appeal to it. There was also a lot of the don't-fuss-with-Mother-Nature wisdom in this notion of the mandate. The Chinese believed that nature sends warnings. The ecological symptoms listed in chapter 1 would be signals that the mandate of heaven is being violated and further ruin awaits us. If toxins are filling your bodies, strange diseases like AIDS are sprouting, sperm counts are declining, ferocious storms are devastating the earth, take heed. The Mandate of Heaven will not be mocked. "The inferior person," said Confucius, "is ignorant of the Mandate of Heaven and does not stand in awe of it." Think of the horror if most of the human race "is ignorant of the Mandate of Heaven and does not stand in awe of it." Would that not be a fair description of the current earth-ravaging humanity?

One Chinese saying puts it this way, "Curses and blessing do not come though the door uninvited. Human beings invite their arrival. The reward of good and evil is like the shadow accompanying a body, and so it is apparent that heaven and earth are possessed of crime-recording spirits." In other words, you can't hide from reckless living. The effects follow you the way your shadow follows your body. For example, if you keep smoking, the crime-recording spirits will bring you to a day of reckoning. Heaven and earth keep records; they record our crimes and punish us for them.

There is a lot of realism in this teaching. If anything, it is more relevant today than it ever was, now that our capacity to destroy exceeds the earth's capacity to heal. A humanity filled with *jen* and reverence for the Mandate of Heaven would make a garden of this earth. The alternative is to make of it a garbage heap. And we will pay the price in disease and pain. Our shadow follows us.

Chinese Hope for Humanity

So when the ancient Chinese pondered human nature and its capacity for self-destruction, did they end up as pure pessimists? Interestingly, they did not. There was a strong belief in this tradition that the Mandate of Heaven, which is marked by compassion and respect for everything in the universe, is imprinted in our nature. Remember, the tao, the *way,* is the basic, primeval wisdom of reality. From this root comes the Mandate of Heaven, and some of it seeps down into our natures. Our job is to look for it and nourish it. Good rulers and good teachers should know that there is some indestructible good at the center of human life and reach for it. We're not all bad. We're a mess, but we are not a hopeless mess because there are tracings of the tao and the Mandate of Heaven in our hearts.

The famous teacher Mencius, living hundreds of years before Jesus, used the example of the spontaneous alarm and distress we feel when we see a child about to fall into a well. That proves, he said, that all of us have "a mind which cannot bear to see the suffering of others." Wang Yang-ming, a thousand years after Mencius, held on to this confidence in humanity and its ability to revive. He wrote: "A great person regards Heaven, Earth, and the myriad things as one body. Such a person regards the world as one family and regards the nation as one person. Those who make a cleavage between objects and distinguish between the self and others are small people." Once we realize that we are all of basically one nature, made from the same *ch'i,* compassion comes naturally to us.

Wang Yang-ming knows that this will seem naive to some people, so he argues his case about our basic goodness. Our distress at seeing a child in mortal danger might be due to the fact that the child is of our same human nature. But, he argues, when a person observes the pitiful cries and frightened appearance of birds and animals about to be slaughtered, we can't ignore a kind of inability to bear their suffering. We cannot view it with indifference. Aha, he says, this shows that deep down we know that we form one body with the birds and animals. But if the cynic says, We feel compassion for them because we know they are sentient like us and share the experience of pain, Wang goes further and says that when we see plants being wantonly destroyed, we can't escape a sense of regret and even pity. That shows we are of one body with the plants too. And finally, he says that when we see the rude shattering of tiles and stones, we cannot stifle all feeling of regret. This means that our minds know implicitly that we are of one body with the tiles and the stones and indeed with everything in the universe.

This hopefulness about human nature has been shared by powerful thinkers and political actors into modern times. Dag Hammarskjöld pondered the reformability of humankind. He looked at the prophet Jesus and noted how he managed to influence some fairly tough "publicans and sinners." How did Jesus pull this off? Hammarskjöld gives the answer in question form: "Was his humanity rich and deep enough to make contact, even in them, with that in human nature which is common to all human beings, something indestructible, and upon which the future has to be built?" The Jewish theologian Martin Buber in the same spirit said that we can give ourselves totally to that which is good but not totally to that which is evil. Yes, the Chinese would say. Exactly. The reflection of the tao and its Mandate of Heaven is in us. The light of the mandate penetrates even the darkness of our egoism. Reach for it, all you who teach and preach and all you who govern.

There is another proof of this hopeful view of humanity. Competition and hostility do not bring us peace. That is yet another sign that the wisdom of tao and the reflection of the Mandate of Heaven are sketched, however dimly, on our minds. When we don't have peace, we experience what doctors call stress, and it tears us apart, causing ulcers and heart attacks. The Mandate of Heaven commands truthfulness, and doesn't the lie detector show that truth is natural to us, that lies trigger reactions that can be measured by the polygraph? Also, although we resist it, benevolence toward others, concern for the poor and the needy, is something we admire. The mandate is in us. It is, of course, sullied. One Confucian writer, Ch'eng, compares it to water that started out clear and pure but got dirtied on its way to the sea. We have to be constantly cleaning up that water, or it will stay turbid and muddy; still, it can be cleaned.

The Chinese tradition put a lot of stress on education and on government. Some traditions, like some forms of Buddhism, have been more concerned with individual solutions to problems. The mainstream of China was not. It was very concerned with what the emperor was doing. It saw government as playing an essential role in realizing the Mandate of

Heaven. That is why the emperor who was not compassionate could get kicked out. Governments that forget the Mandate of Heaven tend to serve only the interests of the overclass, ignoring the needs of the underclass. That is a violation, and the result will be discord; even the overclass will not be at peace. The Chinese conviction was that if you try to enjoy your affluence while ignoring the poverty of others, it won't work. It is simply not the way, the tao, and you and your children will pay the price. Neither government nor education can function successfully for long outside the Mandate of Heaven.

Confucius coined what has been called the Silver Rule: *Do not do to others what you do not want them to do to you.* He put this a little more positively when he said, "Humane persons, desiring to be established themselves, seek to establish others; desiring success for themselves, they help others to succeed. To judge others by what one knows of oneself is the method of achieving humanity." If we applied that to people living in the so-called third world, we would know that they don't desire a life in filth and poverty any more than we would. Inner-city people don't want to live in battered neighborhoods with empty factories and boarded-up buildings any more than we would. Truly humane people would seek governmental policies that would establish these peoples as we ourselves want to be. Add to this Silver Rule the Shadow Rule: if we don't do this, if we are not humane, the effects will come after us. Our criminal indifference will not let us live in peace. The effects of poverty coldly and brutally ignored will follow us into our gated communities and gated nations.

This Chinese belief that we and everything else on the planet are made of the same stuff and are children of heaven and earth affected their ecological ethics. The Christian Saint Augustine said that if we have to go to war and kill people, we should do so "in a mournful mood." The Chinese felt the same way about killing plants and animals even to sustain life for ourselves. At one point in Chinese history, it was legally stipulated that on the first, fifth, and ninth months of the year, as well as on the six fasting days of every month, no one should kill any living being. Fishing and hunting were suspended during these times. This was medicinal, helping people not to take the gifts of nature for granted.

In times past in China, there were popular movements known as "societies for the release of life," which were dedicated to releasing captured animals back into the wild. Since this would be quite problematic in modern conditions, there has been an effort to redirect this compassion into environmental clean-up, a benefit to all forms of life. This is an important development because it shows that the ecological sensitivity of these religions can find new application today in practical ways.

A modern example of this is found in a Chinese Buddhist nun in Taiwan, Cheng-yen, who started up an organization called the Merit Association of Compassion and Relief. She began with four other women in 1963. Deeply distressed by the lack of good medical facilities for the poor, Cheng-yen started to raise money. Many other women joined her, and within twenty years they had raised enough money to open the first Buddhist hospital in Hua-lien in 1986. This hospital would treat any patient regardless of whether she or he had the money to pay. In 1989, they opened a nursing college and, in 1994, a school of medicine. Governments and corporations began to contribute to this, and there are now more than 3.5 million regular members of the association; their work now extends beyond Taiwan to Malaysia, Singapore, Hong Kong, Japan, Australia, England, Austria, South Africa, some South American countries, Canada, and twelve cities in the United States. This is an exciting example of the creative reform needed in all religions. It is based on practical means to express the compassion that is the heart of all the great religions. As Chun-fang Yu says, "it is never easy to change one's way of thinking and one's lifestyle, but time for complacency is running out. Unless a new vision of the earth and human life is formed, the earth will be so damaged that life will not be worth living before too long. To choose not to do so is to fail one's Mandate of Heaven."

Like all moral and religious traditions, the Chinese religions are not perfect. That is why the religions of the world have to get together, to make up for one another's deficiencies. For example, the notion of human rights which is so effective in fighting tyranny was not part of the Chinese legacy. Indeed, there is no word in Chinese that is the exact equivalent of *rights*. As Professor Julia Ching says, the Chinese see in the West an

> excessive individualism and a litigious spirit promoting conflict rather than harmony and an increasing gap between rich and poor in capitalist societies. East Asians value what they call humaneness, or human warmth, which they find lacking in a system where human relationships have lost a personal touch. The West may yet have something to learn from the East.

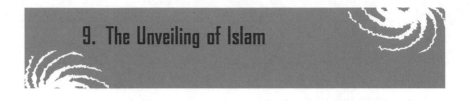

9. The Unveiling of Islam

WRITING IN *Newsweek,* THE COLUMNIST MEG GREENFIELD said: "No part of the world is more hopelessly and systematically and stubbornly misunderstood by us than that complex of religion, culture, and geography known as Islam." She was right, and she was writing over twenty years ago. Since then, Western attitudes toward Islam are even more distorted. We read regularly about holy wars started by Islamic fundamentalists, and we see in Afghanistan the horrific doings of the Taliban, persecuting women and confining them to their homes. Similarly, so-called honor killings of women in Pakistan and elsewhere are attributed by the perpetrators to the teaching of Islam. What guidance, therefore, could we seek from a religion that bears such poisonous fruit?

What we don't see in the newspapers or on television is the impressive historical record of Islam, the powerful teachings on justice and compassion found in the Qu'ran (often written Koran), and the daily life and lifestyle of most Muslims. One out of every five or six people on the planet is a Muslim. We should want to know more about them. Technology has made all people neighbors.

Christians and Jews are often the least informed about the true nature of Islamic faith and history. To make things worse, all religions are inclined to look only at that which is good in their traditions and brush aside the infidelities that fill all faith systems. Jews can point with pride to the stirring words of Micah, the prophet: "[God] has told you . . . what is good; and what does the Lord ask of you but to do justice, and to love kindness, and to walk humbly with your God" (6:8). That's the ideal, but the very same Micah points out how dead those ideals were for many Israelites: "you who hate the good and love the evil, who tear the skin off my people, and the flesh off their bones; who eat the flesh of my people, flay their skin off them, break their bones in pieces and chop them up like meat in a kettle, like flesh in a caldron" (3:1-3). Not much loving kindness or acting justly there. Back then, as today, all people in all religions talked a good game, but the record is often disgraceful. Moral progress gets made. Enlivening insights are born but quickly swallowed up in our mean-spirited smallness.

Before Christians point any fingers at either Muslims or Jews, they should look at the classic words of Jesus in the Sermon on the Mount: "Blessed are the meek . . . Blessed are the merciful . . . Blessed are the pure in heart . . . Blessed are the peacemakers . . ." People who buy that must be the gentlest people on earth. But wait. It was Christians who wrote these words during the Crusades:

> Some of our men cut off the heads of their enemies; others tortured them longer by casting them into the flames. Piles of heads, hands, and feet were to be seen in the streets of the city. In the temple and portico of Solomon, men rode in blood up to their knees and the bridle reins. This day, I say, marks the justification of all Christianity and the humiliation of paganism."

And modern Christians have led the way in supporting slavery and apartheid and in defending bloated military budgets that make the rich richer and the poor more desperate. So let none of us present ourselves in self-righteous postures. All the religions represented in this world tour were born of great visions, and yet their histories are filled with infidelities and violence. Honesty and humility are the necessary passports into interreligious dialogue.

Toward the Real Islam

A chastening walk through history is good therapy for Europeans and Americans. While Christian culture lapsed into what historians call accurately the barbarities of the Dark Ages, Islam was sparkling intellectually. As Huston Smith, the great expert on world religions, writes, "during Europe's Dark Ages, Muslim philosophers and scientists kept the lamp of learning bright, ready to spark the Western mind when it roused from its long sleep." At this point, Islam led the earth in science, largely because of its belief in the reality that God must make sense and should be studied.

Muhammad is considered by many to be the most influential person in human history. Not only was he a religious reformer; he was also a political leader. He was born in the year 570 C.E. into an Arabian world that was in chaos—moral, economic, and political chaos. In his lifetime, he created a unified Arab empire that extended further than Rome or Greece did at their greatest. Had the forces of Islam not been stopped by Charles Martel in 733 in France, all of us Westerners might well be Muslims today!

Yet Muhammad's main achievement was not political or military. It was moral. The times before Muhammad came to be known in Islam as "the days of ignorance." And that put it mildly. Social chaos was the order—or disorder—of the day. Cruelty and wild disparities of wealth, drunkenness, violence, infanticide—especially of girls, and treatment of women as subhuman—all of this was common. In one of the greatest and fastest moral revolutions of history, much of this was turned around within fifty years. It was not turned into a golden age, but a new moral climate was inaugurated. Many of the weak spots of Islamic teaching have to be seen against this background. Often, what looks bad to us was an improvement over what had been. Moral progress is a process from bad to less bad and then to good.

Our special tour guide as we look into the spiritual and moral soul of Islam is a gentle scholar named Nawal Ammar. She is a native of Egypt to which she frequently returns, though now she lives and teaches in the United States at Kent State University. She is one of the founders of the Alliance for Arab Women in Egypt. Ammar writes out of concern for "the crisis of an earth bleeding and burning" in order to accommodate a fivefold economic expansion in just the last forty years. Many of us are doing well in that expansion, but the earth must be wondering how much more of this kind of prosperity it can bear. Professor Ammar knows the problem is not specific to Muslims, but "the manifestations of the crisis in Muslim communities and countries are as alarming as anywhere else in the world and illustrate some of the problems that afflict other religions." As with all the other tour guides through the world religions in this book, Ammar wants to show the *shareable wisdom* found in her faith community and to help us experience some of the help she has found in Islam.

Islam, more than any other religion, is a religion of the book. The book is the Qu'ran and as the Qu'ran puts it, the Lord "teaches by the pen." The Qu'ran is for devout Muslims what Jesus is to orthodox Christians. It is divine. No book has ever shaped a culture the way that book has shaped the vast expanse of nations that call themselves Islam.

Muslims do not feel that the wisdom revealed to Muhammad was the only revelation in history. Indeed, Muslims feel the Qu'ran is the culmination of a series of revelations begun with Abraham. (That is why Judaism, Christianity, and Islam are often referred to as the Abrahamic religions; all trace back to Abraham as the root.) Islam believes that God revealed monotheism to Abraham, the Ten Commandments to Moses, the Golden Rule of doing to others as we would have them do unto us to Jesus. All these were authentic revelations, but the revelation to Muhammad was the grand finale. This definitive revelation was also more specific. The Golden Rule is not enough. You need to plunge right in to the specifics of human relationships and economics and politics to make a faith live. That's what the Qu'ran does. Other sayings of Muhammad, known as *hadith,* have been passed down, but to be accepted as authentic, they must not contradict the Qu'ran. Other laws and traditions developed over the centuries, known as *shariah,* are very influential in modern Islam, and, unfortunately, many of these are highly sexist and used to justify the horrible treatment of women by groups such as the Taliban. These hateful practices and those parts of *shariah* do not pass the Qu'ranic test and cannot be considered genuinely Islamic.

Islam, however, is not just a matter of reading. It also mandates thinking. Knowledge is highly esteemed. That's why philosophy and science prospered in early Islam. As the Qu'ran puts it in a rhetorical question: "Are those who know equal to those who do not know!" It has been said by

Christians that what is necessary to make your way through life is to have a good newspaper in one hand and the Bible in the other. Muslims can agree with that. See what the Qu'ran has to say, look at the world in all its complexity and study, study, study, . . . and then do something about it. That is the Islamic mandate. The Christian Teilhard de Chardin said that study (research) is a form of worship and, again, Muslims would heartily agree. The universe is God's handwork. The study and enhancement of it is a religious duty.

Who's in Charge?

The mainstream of Islam never believed that whatever will be will be. History does not follow a predestined path. We make it or break it. The ecological and economic crises we address in this book are not just our lot in life, to be accepted with true grit and patience. If it's a mess, we made it. It's our mess. As we saw also in the religions of India and China, historical crises for Islam are always moral crises at root and susceptible to reform. A crisis is a call to action. When things go disastrously wrong, the Muslim tendency is to look to greed, human injustice, lack of moderation, and lack of respect for God's creation. The ultimate sin is to believe in what David Loy called "the religion of the market" and not to believe in Allah, the God of justice and compassion. Nawal Ammar condemns the Gulf War, which was waged by the West against Iraq. She sees it as a war of greed, an oil war intended to preserve our greedy lifestyle. Some 200,000 people were killed and injured. Thousands of Kurds were displaced. Most of the so-called precision bombs missed their targets. The Iraqis conducted war on nature by burning oil wells, obstructing the sunlight, affecting the ozone layer in the northern hemisphere, and poisoning people, including Allied soldiers. This is not just politics as usual. This is savagery, a breakdown of politics, and a pathetic portrait of humanity at its worst. It is sin at work, not heroism. That is how this Egyptian Muslim sees it.

If religion was at work here, it was the religion of the market, clearing the way for the god called consumption. President Bush said that our "lifestyle" was at stake. Yes, our overconsuming, gluttonous lifestyle.

Professor Ammar admits with sorrow that many Muslims are not giving good examples of their faith in caring for the earth. There is a water crisis in Islamic countries. Dumping waste into rivers, seas, and streams is common, and the states seem ineffective in controlling it. Explosives are used for fishing, destroying the habitat. Leaded gasoline is used, which finds its way into drinking water. The air in Cairo is ten times more polluted than a city equal to its size in the United States. Islamic countries are the major holders of oil reserves in the world, but, she says, "the extraction of oil and its by-products is undertaken with minimal controls on toxic emissions and hazards." The Muslim faith teaches that wealth, in the form of money, property, or resources, is a trust given to us by God to be used gently and generously to advance God's creative purposes.

Solutions

A journey through other religions is also a journey through other languages. We meet words that have no parallel in English, and yet they are repositories and sanctuaries of wisdom and experience. They are words worth knowing. Ammar introduces us first to *hay'a,* and she says right off that it houses meaning that will not fit tidily into any of our existing English words. It is a word that reflects a kind of respectful shyness, deference, and reverence. It is not a shyness that proceeds from fear but from appreciation. It is a kind of humility in the face of excellence. *Hay'a* is also a word full of concern, a concern for God's glory as reflected in creation and in all other creatures. It is the opposite of the Greek *hubris,* meaning "arrogant pride and self-centeredness."

Ammar says quite simply that it is the absence of *hay'a* that is causing the world's ecological crisis. The absence of *hay'a* in Islam and in the rest of the world is the cause of the disparity between rich and poor, the success of corporations in stimulating overconsumption and the maldistribution of resources, wars, the intolerance of ethnic diversity, oppression of women, infant mortality, and crime.

Hay'a is the virtue that gives Islam its reputation for tolerance and acceptance. Though Islam lived in a tough world and was more than ready to fight its enemies, the Qu'ran calls Muslims to tolerance. Muhammad was known for being gentle and merciful even to his enemies. It is not surprising that African Americans have been drawn to Islam. We think of Kareem Abdul-Jabbar, the basketball player, and Muhammad Ali, the boxer. They did not find the prejudice there that they found among all too many Christians. There are 120 verses in the Qu'ran ordering Muslims to respect all non-Muslims. The diversity of humans was seen to be God's delight. God says, "We have indeed created humans in the best mold." Difference and diversity are seen to be God's will in Islam, not grounds for discrimination.

This story is told of the prophet Muhammad:

> Upon the passing of a funeral procession near where the Prophet gathered with some of his friends, he stood up in respect, and so did the rest of them gathered. After the procession passed, one person in the crowd said: "O Messenger of God, did you know that this was the funeral of a Jew?" The Prophet replied: "Wasn't he human and had a human soul? Was he not a human created and made by God? Wasn't he a being with dignity?"

In the same spirit, the instruction given to a Muslim ruler was this: "Fill your heart with mercy and love to your subjects since they are of two kinds: a sibling in belief (i.e., a Muslim) or a human created by God the same way you were." The Muslim and non-Muslim have equal human rights.

Hay'a is an attitude of grateful reverence. It connects with the well-known obligation of Muslims to pray five times a day. The main motive for prayer is not to be asking for favors of God but to express gratitude for the gift of existence that has been given. The psychology here is interesting because it recognizes our tendency to take it all for granted and to lose all perspective. So Muslims are told to get back on their knees and to remember how blessed they are. If you don't do it five times a day, you are going to forget.

Muslims do not think we are a hopeless species. In fact, they are more hopeful about humanity than many Christians. They have no doctrine of original sin, a rather pessimistic doctrine that almost seems to see depravity as destiny for our species. The Muslims think that, as bad as we are, God can make something of us. In this hope, they are closer to Catholic Christians than to Protestant Christians. Catholic theology showed strong confidence in grace—a confidence that some Protestant theologians have called naïve—but Islam would come in on the Catholic side. Buddhism and the Chinese religions would also be comfortable with this kind of guarded optimism. Islam would also be open to the observation of the orthodox Jewish scholar Martin Buber. Buber said we can give ourselves over totally to that which is good; we cannot give ourselves totally to that which is evil. One has to hope that Buber and the Muslims are right because it would inspire more courageous efforts for reform.

The Qu'ran and Economics 101

Remember that Islam sees the moral revelations to Israel and to Christianity as basically true but not detailed enough. That is why God had to send another prophet, Muhammad, to give detailed instructions on how to live. Islamic revelation jumps into economics, and the first lesson in Islamic economics is *poverty;* the message is: "Get rid of it!" This is very much like Deuteronomy in the Hebrew Bible: "There will . . . be no one in need among you" (15:4). Poverty is seen as a human failure in caring and sharing. It's not just fate. There is human skullduggery involved, and like Jews and Christians, the Muslims tilt the blame mostly toward the rich and powerful, not toward the poor folks. Remember, for Muslims, the Qu'ran is God talking. And guess what God says? Taxes!

Nobody likes taxes. Why does God like them? Professor Ammar gives us the answer: "All taxes aim to redistribute the wealth and power of the rich to the poor." Are they recommending communism? No. As Ammar says, the purpose of the law is to create a society "of private ownership and enterprise without the vast accumulation and concentration of wealth." As she says, it is a kind of third way between laissez-faire capitalism and communism. Here is the way Islamic taxing works.

The tax on Muslims is the strictest. It is a yearly tax of 2.5 percent on all that you possess—not on all that you earn. In other words, you have to give one-fortieth of all that you possess, and this is "a religious obligation intended for the rich to fulfill the needs of the poor in the community." Some Islamic jurists add that if this tax is not enough to meet all the demands of the poor, the tax rate may be increased. The tax is based on need. As long as there is need, people must share, and this is seen as the will of God, the Great Giver of everything that we have. Those who are making money from the land and its resources must pay the tax on "the gross production before deduction of production costs," according to Professor Ammar. This system of taxation, says Professor Ammar, is "an economic mechanism for limiting the disparities in access to resources" which unregulated trade would generate.

And Islam is right. Unregulated trade, often referred to by smart people as neoliberal economics, creates weird and unjust disparities. Margaret Thatcher, former British prime minister, was a firm believer in this system of economics, and it did just what the Muslims say it does. Before Thatcher, about one British person in ten was living below the poverty line. After Thatcher, one person in four is poor, and one child in three falls below the poverty line. Those with high salaries got tax reductions, and those with low salaries got tax increases. Islam has a word for this: they call it *sin*.

Ronald Reagan also was enamored of this kind of economics. Kevin Philips, a Republican analyst and former aide to President Nixon, wrote about the Reagan changes. Over the decade of the 1980s, the top 10 percent of American families increased their average family income by 16 percent; the top 5 percent increased by 23 percent; and the awfully lucky top 1 percent increased their income by 50 percent due to tax breaks. The bottom 10 percent saw their income drop by 10 percent. Again, the Muslim word for that is sin. What such systems lack is what Ammar calls "an economic mechanism for limiting the disparities in access to resources." Exactly.

Islamic economics also forbids the taking of interest in the way our Western economics uses interest. When a bank gives a loan, it is guaranteed return on that loan even if the business you borrowed it for fails. Islamic teaching requires that borrower and entrepreneur share both the risks and the profits. Our system of one party being guaranteed a profit is seen as normal by us, as immoral by them. There is a fear in Islamic thinking of the powerful taking advantage of the weak. Would any of us call that unrealistic?

Islam does not encourage sloth. There is a strong emphasis on the importance and the dignity of work. The Qu'ran says: "Humans shall have nothing but what they strive for." If you can't find work, they will take care of you, but work has an important place in God's plan.

Exchange should be based on real value, not on artificially superimposed value. Nawal Ammar gives an example of what Islam is condemning here. She tells this story: "In 1996, a toy called 'Tickle Me Elmo' (a Sesame Street figure) usually sold for $26, but it became so rare that some people were auctioning it for over $1,500." Ammar says: "This kind of exchange that is based on creating an artificial need and crazed desire is not permitted in the Islamic system." This can be a little embarrassing for us in our system. Fake value is everywhere. A watch is wonderful for telling time, so in our system we load the watch with other prestige values on top of telling time, and all of a sudden people are paying thousands of dollars for elite big-name watches, some of them made of nothing more precious than stainless steel! (One friend of mine was given such a watch. He occasionally has to take it in for repairs, and in the meantime he uses his old cheap Timex that has not needed repairs!) It is well known that certain prestige automobiles are basically the same car as a lower-priced model from the same company, with a different top. (I'll avoid lawsuits by not mentioning them, but any informed mechanic will confirm this.) This is silly and dumb. It is almost like a drug, a show-off drug, where people get high on displaying their wealth. Islam would add that it is also immoral in a world filled with poverty.

Good Government

Talk about a counterculture. Islam is that. We can see Islam as a source of helpful criticism. Their view of economics basically tells us that we practice a kind of Robin Hood–style economics in reverse: take from the poor, and give to the rich. They also have lessons for us on the nature of government. We in Europe and North America live in nations where government is portrayed as an evil. Tom Paine, the early American pamphleteer, said government is a "necessary evil." Many Americans agree. You can get elected to government in the United States by running against government! Of course, we are not consistent in this. When corporations get into trouble, they go running like crybabies to the government to bail them out. Most welfare goes to the rich, not to the poor, in the form of corporate welfare.

Islam knows that government, in whatever form, is a basic human necessity, and that government has positive roles to play to keep life livable. You will remember Harold Coward's concept of the we-self. Islam encourages a strong sense of community and of human solidarity. The civic ideal is a united people free of oppression. Government is not the only agency to bring that about, but it is the principal agency. It has more carrot and more stick and thus more power. And its business is not profit and growth. Its business is protecting the common good. As Ammar says, "In Islam the leader has no divine powers. The legitimacy of the Muslim leader is based on the will of the community according to Islamic jurisprudence." Justice, equality, and humility (of all things!) are the marks of a good leader and of good government. Government that is not obeying God's law of justice, compassion, and care of the poor and is not promoting peace (the word *Islam* means "peace") is not legitimate government and need not be obeyed.

Good economics involves good government. Over fifty years ago, the economic theorist Karl Polanyi made this statement: "To allow the market mechanism to be the sole director of the fate of human beings and their natural environment . . . would result in the demolition of society." That's simple wisdom, and Polanyi was a prophet. When corporations overrun government, as they are doing now, the poor and the environment are demolished. *Demolition* was not too strong a word to describe what is going on. (Refer back to chapter 1 for the gory data.)

Any sensitive theory of economics and of human well-being cannot ignore the question of how many people a finite earth can support. Islam, like all the major religions, was born at a time when overpopulation was not a problem. Staying alive and seeing some of your kids survive was the challenge, so we don't look to ancient religions for a spelled-out family planning program. It is not surprising, therefore, to hear from Professor Ammar that the birthrate of the forty-six Muslim countries is 1 percent higher than that of the so-called third world as a whole. Islam, however, like the other religions, is full of commonsense approaches to problems. If you have problems, work on them. Having more people than the land can support is a problem. Family planning programs have been started as national policy in many Muslim lands and have had remarkable success in one of them, Indonesia. Ammar notes that Islam stresses "the quality and not the quantity of children."

As the jurist and Islamic expert Azizah Al-Hibri writes: "The majority view among Muslim scholars on contraception has been that it is permissible with the wife's consent." And, on abortion, she reports: "The majority of Muslim scholars permit abortion, although they differ on the stage of fetal development beyond which it becomes prohibited." As Professor Ammar observes, as women get educated and find employment, they delay marriage and limit births. The educational and economic empowerment of women is, as always, the best birth control.

What about the Women?

Anyone who reads the newspapers knows that women have problems in Islam. Muslim scholars do not hide from this. Muslim feminist Fatima Mernissi says that Muslim society was organized so that "the male citizens . . . possessed among other things the female half of the population." Men had more rights and privileges than Muslim women, "including even the right to kill their women." Riffat Hassan, a Muslim scholar from Pakistan now at the University of Louisville, says this rests on the idea that women "have been created mainly to be of use to men who are superior to them."

Although polygamy has been permitted in Islam, it is less prevalent than in times past. Polygamy meant that you had to marry your female sexual partner, not just use and discard her as had been done in pre-Islamic times. Polygamy was in effect an intermediate improvement over the horrible exploitation of women that preceded Islam. With education today and with the growth in understanding of women as fully fledged persons, this practice is abating. Women in Islam with educational and economic opportunities are less subjected to the indignity of polygamy. Ammar tells us that in Egypt only 0.01 percent of women with university degrees are in polygamous unions. Education is the solvent of this social evil.

Muslim scholars are now showing that the oppression of women is a deviation from the true spirit of the Qu'ran. "If any do deeds of righteousness, be they male or female, and have faith, they will enter Heaven, and not the least injustice will be done to them." "Men and women are protectors, one of another." There are other texts like that. Denying women rights equal to men's is an injustice and a violation of the will of God. That is true Islamic orthodoxy. Early Islam was to a degree a women's liberation movement. Women could own property in their own name—a revolutionary advance at that time. As Huston Smith points out, that is a right that was not enjoyed by women in the United States until the twentieth century. Women in modern Islam have also risen to be prime ministers and party leaders. There are women's rights movements even in the conservative Islamic Republic of Iran, fueled by Qu'ranic and other religious sources. The reform is under way.

10. Judaism:
Workshop for a New Humanity

JUDAISM BEGAN AS A MORAL REVOLUTION, perhaps the most successful and influential revolution in human history. It did not look all that promising at its start, way back some three thousand years ago. The dramatis personae were a ragtag but highly gifted bunch of escaped slaves out of Egypt, some nomads and wandering shepherds and misfits from the surrounding stable societies in that part of the world. Disgusted by what they saw in the kingdoms around them, they rethought life, with its politics and economics, from the bottom up, and there is no one in the Western world who is not the beneficiary of that rethinking.

Our guide on our visit to Judaism is Professor Laurie Zoloth, who teaches at San Francisco State University. She is living proof that with focused energy and discipline, women as well as men can be happy parents of five children and still become leading professionals in their fields. Her field is ethics and religion, with particular concentration in her religion, orthodox Judaism. A thoroughly observant and faithful Jew, Zoloth is a student of all the world's religions. She demonstrates that you can be committed to one religion and yet open to the wisdom in all. Indeed, Professor Zoloth's special talent is in showing the messages in Judaism that can speak meaningfully to people of all faiths and persuasions. And that is what this book is all about. Truth is never prisoner to a monopoly. It is shareable, and it crops up literally everywhere. Good ideas and ideals need no passports to enter an open mind.

It is remarkable that little Israel had the influence it did. As scripture scholar Morton Smith said: "This small country during this brief period became the seedbed of the subsequent religious history of the Western world." Israel was a prolific parent. Its two children are Christianity and Islam, though, as is often the case, children do not appreciate their debt to their parents. Even today, Judaism is a numerically small religion. Zoloth reminds us that in the whole world there are only thirteen million Jews, and in the United States, Jews are only 2 percent of the population. How, then, have their ideas spread across the planet? She replies by quoting Zechariah 4:6: "Not by might, and not by power but by *ruach alone!*" *Ruach* means "spirit," "breath," including the breath of speech. Israel told its story and did so eloquently. Literary talent was one key to their success. Writing was still a new art in the human community, but these folks were into it. Early Israel was, in fact, a literary as well as a moral revolution. Indeed, in many parts of the United States, you cannot check into a hotel without finding a copy of their writings in your nightstand drawer, and presidents and popes are sworn into office by putting their hands on those ancient Hebrew writings. Judaism, Christianity, and Islam are called the three Abrahamic religions, and it is no surprise that their members are also known as "people of the book."

The Significance of Exile

There is an extraordinary religious and moral richness in Judaism, and we will touch on as much of it as we can, but Laurie Zoloth selects a master theme: *exile*. She says it was the Hebrew experience of exodus and exile that set the tone for Jewish spirituality. It also gave Israel a way of explaining the plight and the promise of all of us mortals who dwell upon this lovely earth. What she is saying, and I think her insight here is quite original, is based on the story of Adam and Eve being exiled from the Garden of Eden, Cain being exiled from everywhere, and the Jewish people being exiled from their own country in Babylonian captivity. All this banishment is actually "metaphorically applicable to all peoples." For the whole human race, paradise has been lost. We are all a people alienated from our true destiny. It has not yet appeared what we can be.

To understand this, it helps to realize with biblical scholars that the story of the garden in Genesis is a vision of the future, not a description of a past. There was no garden.

What there was for the poetic authors of the Genesis stories was a vision of a world that could be, where people would live in harmony with one another, with all of nature, and with God. Our history and our isolating egoism exile us from this possibility, but we are tortured by the fact that we know it could be.

Laurie Zoloth expresses this exile experience in language that is pure poetry.

> Adamic exile is a nakedness beyond naming, a stripping of all but the scent of Paradise, carried on the animal skins of Adam and Eve, later in the skins of Esau that Jacob steals, later on the coat of Joseph, a scent which will reemerge again and again in the world of rabbinic writing . . . a hint of the infinite possibility of a world healed.

This is the panhuman experience. Here we are, "a humanity that searches for home in a fragile modern world. We are both lost and at fault, at risk and accountable, bearers of the scent of Paradise and lovers of the pleasure of the desert, easily seduced by idols, losing track of the column of fire in the night." No longer is this the Jewish story; this is human history. We are heading for a promised land, but we are not there yet. Look back to chapter 1 of this book, where I described in some gory detail the mess we have made of society and the planet. This is not the promised land. Not yet. Even the exodus does not end in the promised land, "but on the shores of the Jordan, the home is in sight, but not entered."

Zoloth is not talking here about a plot of land in the Middle East called Palestine and Israel. That misses the point. The promised land is a parable of possibility, and we are the exiles stumbling toward it.

What makes this Jewish experience so powerful and so applicable to us is that "Jewish history is framed by narrow escapes from total annihilation. . . . European Jews experience life in a period of total environmental collapse, a near species extinction." That is what makes Jewish experience exportable to the rest of humanity. The nuclear weaponry readied in our arsenals can achieve species extinction, creating a world where only cockroaches could survive. The poisoning of the essential elements of life threaten our species as we rapidly go about extinguishing other innocent species. This is a desert experience, as dangerous and hostile as the desert was to the ancient Hebrews. The desert we have made is "a world full of lost chances . . . fundamentally unredeemed but redeemable."

Laurie Zoloth finds hope in the desert experience, and hope is what we need. She said the "forty years in the desert was to burn out the slave in the bone." Maybe some of our suicidal weirdness is getting burned out of our bones as we see the wreck of a planet that was healthier before we came. Maybe. And yet, with the typical Jewish sense of paradox, Zoloth worries and wonders, "If persons of faith do not call the ethical question, if we too are lulled into a somnambulant despair by the pursuit of commodities, the coolness of the silk on our cheeks, the pleasure of the company we keep, and that company's proximity to power, then who will?" If people who believe that God loves us and the earth "with an everlasting love," that God made the earth and invited us to cherish it and one another in loving union with God—if people stirred by such a faith do not rise to the crisis on earth, "then who will?" That's Zoloth's question and the question of Jewish faith to all who call themselves people of faith.

Judaism's Grand Paradox

Part of Jewish wisdom is the recognition that paradox, not clarity, is often the mark of truth. When you see things too clearly and unambiguously, you may not be seeing them at all. In one striking example of paradox, Judaism seems to affirm both unparalleled despair and unique hope for the human race. Laurie Zoloth speaks of us as "unredeemed" and "broken." And the Jewish Bible is even harsher. "The LORD looks down from heaven on humankind to see if there are any who are wise. . . . They have all gone astray, they are all alike perverse; there is no one who does good, no, not one" (Ps. 14:2-3). That is a fairly sweeping indictment. "We have all become like one who is unclean, and all our righteous deeds are like a filthy cloth" (Isa. 64:6). Not flattering!

Can we improve? Jeremiah doesn't offer much hope. "Can Ethiopians change their skin or leopards their spots? Then also you can do good who are accustomed to do evil" (13:23).

Alongside this stinging diagnosis of our moral state, there arose in Israel a stunningly hopeful vision of what we and life on this earth can be. The futuristic paradise story was the start of that. Life on earth could be a garden of harmony and delight. Then Isaiah put into the mouth of God extravagant promises that imply that we could be remade and develop a demilitarized politics and a humane economic system. Here is poetry at its boldest.

> For I am about to create new heavens and a new earth; the former things shall not be remembered or come to mind. . . . no more shall the sound of weeping be heard in [Jerusalem], or the cry of distress. . . . They shall build houses and inhabit them; they shall plant vineyards and eat their fruit. . . . They shall not labor in vain, or bear children for calamity. . . . The wolf and the lamb shall feed together, the lion shall eat straw like the ox. . . . They shall not hurt or destroy on all my holy mountain, says the Lord. (Isa. 65:17-25)

The holy mountain on which there will be no hurting or destruction is the entire earth. We could be a nonviolent species, Israel believed. Israel is simply the workshop for this new humanity. Israel and its vision of possible peace is to be "a light to the nations, . . . [shining all the way] to the end of the earth" (Isa. 49:6). The experiment was local; the effect was to be global. As the Jewish scripture scholar Jacob Neusner says, the Israelites "believed that history depended upon what happened in the Land of Israel."

Justice as the Price of Peace

The birthing of a new humanity will not happen automatically. There is work to be done. The work is called *justice,* justice to all people and justice to this good earth. Professor Zoloth puts it this way: both nature and humanity need taming. Unlike those who today are called deep ecologists, who romanticize the wildness of nature, Israel said both nature and we need cultivation, nonviolent cultivation. Nature untamed is chaos; it would be no place to raise children. Nature crushed by development is also no place to raise children. As Zoloth says, "It is foolish to waste or ruin the land, to poison or to strip it, but in Jewish thought, it is not morally incorrect to manipulate it."

Part of Jewish wisdom on ecology is ritualized in the Sabbath. Every seventh day was the Sabbath, and every seventh year was the sabbatical year. The Sabbath, in Zoloth's words, was a time "of cessation, of voluntary retreat from the endless possibility of production and consumption." As Rabbi Daniel Fink puts it: "Once a week we are called upon to refrain from all labor that uses the things of nature for the achievement of human ends." On the Sabbath day and the sabbath year, we stop the obsessions of "clattering commerce," step out of the rat race, and remember that we are part of nature, not its lord. The Jewish Bible is crystal clear on that. "The earth is the LORD's," says the psalmist. We are tenants on God's earth, and the Sabbath tells us to sit down and remember that. So the Jewish sense of ecology is a tonic for a modernity drunk on technology.

Jewish justice is a breed apart. It is usually called *sedaqah*, with the accent on the *da*. It is a powerful concept and is the very heart of Jewish spirituality. Someone who practices *sedaqah* is a *sadiq*. Sometimes modern Jews will say in an obituary that the deceased lived a life marked by *sedaqah*. It is the highest compliment that can be paid to a departed brother or sister by the Jewish community. I learned the power of the word once on a train ride from New York to Washington, D.C. I happened to sit next to an elderly rabbi, and it turned the trip into a treat. He was filled with a compassionate and gentle wisdom and wit and was a living example of the truth that morality at its best is beautiful. He was also the soul of Jewish *sedaqah*. As we parted, I said to him, "Sir, you are a *sadiq!*" His response shocked me. He backed up, winced, and shrank from the compliment. I realized that what I had said to him was, in effect, "Sir, you have the heart of God beating in your chest," because that is what *sedaqah* is. It is the very holiness of God, and this gentle soul would lay no claim to that, although he could, in my judgment, do so.

Sedaqah has a rather un-American flavor. For most of us Westerners, justice implies impartiality. We would never say of a judge that she is a great judge but very prejudiced, partial, and biased. But *sedaqah*, Jewish justice, is prejudiced, partial, and biased, and the prejudice is a two-edged sword. It is biased toward the poor and suspicious of the economically secure. *Sedaqah* has built into its etymology the notion of mercy for the poor. The gods are with the mighty, said the Roman Tacitus. Not so, said Israel. Our God is "a God of the humble . . . the poor . . . the weak . . . the desperate . . . and the hopeless" (Jdt. 9:11). The biblical writers believed that financial security can easily corrode the conscience. "Take care. . . . When you have eaten your fill and have built fine houses and live in them, and when your herds and flocks have multiplied, and all that you have is multiplied" (Deut. 8:11-13). All this can lead to haughtiness of heart and forgetfulness of *sedaqah*.

In deciding on any policy, think first of the poor and how it will affect them. Think especially of children. I have always felt that the most comprehensive rule in ethics is this: *what is good for kids is good; what is bad for kids is ungodly.* That squares perfectly with this Jewish view of justice. Think of the kids now living and those yet to be born, and then decide what is good. A lot of debate in Congress and the parliaments of the world could serve us better under that banner.

Sedaqah calls us to be, in Zoloth's words, "sleeplessly responsible" for the poor of the world.

This is the very heart of religion. Isaiah 58 defines religion as helping the overworked, freeing slaves and oppressed people, sharing food with the hungry, providing housing for the homeless poor, clothing the naked, and satisfying the need of the wretched of the earth. When Job defended his virtue, he went right to the *sedaqah* tradition to do it. He didn't say he was a good man because he paid his bills and honored all contracts. That would never satisfy Jewish justice. His defense was that he had been "eyes to the blind, and feet to the lame . . . a father to the needy;" he saved the orphan, the widow, and "the poor who cried for help." He even—and this is crucial—took up the cause of persons whom he did not even know (Job 29:12-20). There is a reason why Jews score higher on concern for the poor in polls taken after elections in the United States.

Solidarity with those in need is the heart of Jewish morality and religion. Remember the image of the human race in exile, in the desert of our own making, yet filled with the scent of paradise, a gnawing sense of the goodness that could be. We are all in diaspora, exiled from our true possibilities. And in this desert, Zoloth says, "it is the obligation toward the stranger that is at your side, and hers to the one at her side, that will make the time in the desert bearable." A sense of solidarity with all that lives, human and not, is the only prescription for saving the earth. Not to practice the compassionate justice of *sedaqah* is "to literally stop the rain." Nothing will grow. Again Zoloth: "It is an absolute organizing principle in Judaism that the community has a stronger appeal than the autonomous individual." And the community includes the rest of biological nature as well as people born and yet to be born. Egoistic, greedy individualism is an unhappy kind of autism, as the ecologist and Catholic theologian Thomas Berry says. Not knowing and feeling our relationship with all that lives and all that is in this blessed corner of the universe is a tragic, autistic isolation.

Such egoistic separateness is sick and unreal. Remember that science believes that all that lives began with a single cell. How else account for the basic similarity in the DNA code and the similar amino acids in all forms of life? We are also not detached from the nonliving elements of the universe. The word *human,* after all, comes from *humus,* meaning "dirt." As Protestant theologian Larry Rasmussen writes: "No clear line between life and nonlife exists." We can breathe due to the gases of now-dead stars that produced oxygen for us. This sense of de facto oneness with all that is should breed an enlivening sense of relatedness; it should also generate compassion for all that is, compassion for the earth and for all people.

If we can learn of the grinding poverty in Haiti and Bangladesh and feel unmoved to action within our possibilities, our consciences are partially dead, and we are to that degree corrupt. As the early feminist Mary Wollstonecraft wrote two hundred years ago: "Those who are able to see pain, unmoved, will soon learn to inflict it." And we do inflict pain, mainly by our apathy.

Judaism, from its start, has been a call from apathy to action, a call to let something of the pathos, the empathy and feeling of God, turn the stone of our hearts into living, breathing, feeling flesh.

Next in our journey, we turn to two more of Israel's influential children: Protestant and Catholic Christianities.

11. Protestant Christianity and the Recovery of Lost Fragrance

IN EACH CHAPTER OF THIS BOOK, WE ARE LOOKING FOR HELP for a wounded humanity on a broken planet. We're looking in the great classics of cherishing that we call the religions of the world. In each of them, there are recoverable energies and ideas that have healing power. Since nothing under the sun is perfect, we know that all religions are also something of a mess. There is a lot of the debris of history and human corruption that seeps into even our finest moments.

Catherine Keller is our principal guide for the journey into Protestant Christianity. She is a professor of theology at Drew University in New Jersey. Her writing, like that of Laurie Zoloth, is full of poetic power. Keller knows that her task is special because of the unparalleled influence of Protestant thought and feeling on the history of the whole world.

The whole world? Isn't that a bit much? Not really. As Professor Keller notes: "Protestants, who constitute a significant mass of the Euro-American majority of that 20 percent of the global population consuming 80 percent of the planet's resources, are a force to be reckoned with." Had China, which was a developed culture long before Europe, staked its imperialistic claim on the world, Confucianism might have been the world-shaping philosophy. That didn't happen. China stayed close to home. The Euro-Americans, when they rose to power, set sail and circled the globe with their vision of life. This invasion continues today with the Internet, by which both the English language and ideas—especially American ideas—spread into the nooks and crannies of the world. Keller rightly sees Protestant ideas as mightily influential on the Euro-American invasion of the world.

What's Wrong with Protestantism?
Before looking into the positives of Protestant Christianity, Keller bluntly confronts the negatives. Her belief is that "a

faith can only cure what it first diagnoses in itself." The poisons in any faith system can only be "adequately countered from within." Protestant honesty has always stressed the confession of guilt. Keller's confessional words: "Any core or nature of Protestantism is rotten with the modern diseases of nation-state and the New World imperialism it acquired so early, and the patriarchy it unquestioningly absorbed." She says further: "Christendom, as the social form of the religion, has been the carrying culture for the colonization of the planet. To this end it has interpreted its theological sources, its manly mandates to populate, dominate, use, and convert the world. If I do Christian theology, I do it in penance for the effects of Christendom." Beat that for candor!

Antinature, Prowork

In her diagnostic surgery, Keller goes straight to the influential Protestant ideas of nature and industriousness. First, to nature.

Keller takes us first to Kierkegaard who in *Either/Or* is writing about Johannes the Seducer. Johannes has been the successful seducer of Cordelia and finally gets to enjoy what he calls his "reward." However, the day after his conquest, he writes: "I do not wish to be reminded of my relation to her; she has lost the fragrance." Keller sees in Johannes's exploitative disenchantment an example of "the standard Protestant theology of nature." Nature has lost its fragrance. Early Protestantism was victimized by an overwhelming concept of original sin, seen as a corruption of all of nature. Nature is no longer the lovely text written by the Creator filled with hints and reflections of that Creator's beauty and goodness. "The manifestation of God in nature speaks to us in vain," said John Calvin. Our eyes are blinded and can only be opened "by the inner revelation of God through faith." Natural theology that sees the earth as "crammed with heaven" (in the words of Jesuit poet Gerard Manly Hopkins) is illusory because, again in Calvin's words, original sin has left "the fault of dullness within us."

Nature, then, is downgraded drastically, and so are we. Again Calvin: "The spirit comes, not from nature, but regeneration." Nature is "flesh," and flesh is hostile to and the opposite of "spirit." This hardly sets the stage for ecological sensitivity. There is a terrible dualism here, a fatal split between us and the rest of nature. Afterlife is what counts, not earth life. Nature is only a stage on which our journey to heaven takes place. You can see why the scientist Lynn White in a famous 1967 essay put the blame for the ecocrisis squarely on Christianity's shoulders. The Christian faith, he said, "bears a huge burden of guilt" because it is "the most anthropocentric religion the world has seen." It operates on the assumption that nature has no purpose other than to serve human needs. Another writer, Donald Worster, says that "Christianity has maintained a calculated indifference, if not antagonism, toward nature." Notice that these writers do not put the blame only on Protestant Christianity but on all Christianity. Note too that even these critics see in Christianity the cure for this bad theology. Saint Francis of Assisi is just one example. And there are Protestant Coleridges to contrast for Kierkegaards. Still, Keller reaches the hard conclusion that Protestantism at its worst "provided the spiritual impetus for the genocidal and ecocidal conquest of North America."

Now bring on the industrial revolution and a capitalism nourished with such human-centered antinature feelings, and nature had better watch out. Nature in this view is nothing but raw material awaiting our use and abuse. And when that form of capitalism goes global, the whole planet is wracked with pain and no longer filled with the glory of God but with the poisons of humankind.

This theology run amuck had even more comfort for imperialists. Again Kierkegaard symbolized the problem. From his Scandinavian perch, he expressed scorn for "the astonishing, the shrieking superlatives of a southern people." He derides their superficial emotions and "astonishment over the vastness of nature and the countless forms of animal life." Those who cherish nature with enthusiasm are "pagans," a term that is code for Catholics in Kierkegaard. Keller berates "such Protestant stereotypes of those sensuous, southern peoples, emotional, outward, and 'natural' in their expressions of wonder." Such disdain, she says, is "ever recognizable just beneath the surface of northern cultures . . . [and] . . . has proved a receptive ground for breeding the wildly materialistic projects of white colonialism against all manner of southern peoples and their material milieus." So nature and those in love with it are both apt subjects for exploitation. Dangerous dynamite to put in the hands of rapacious capitalists. Again, not all capitalists are rapacious; unfortunately, too many are. Protestant readers should not despair at this point. Professor Keller is just giving the bad news first.

It's Off to Work We Go. . . .

Most folks have heard of "the Protestant work ethic" even if they have never read Max Weber's *The Protestant Ethic and the Spirit of Capitalism*. Weber, the sociologist, was trying to figure out what makes capitalism tick, and he saw a huge Protestant influence. The Puritan tradition stressed hard, continuous labor as the best defense against the weakness of the flesh. Calvin didn't even think you should take Christmas Day off from work. A life of hard, disciplined work was the best remedy against the proclivities of our fallen nature. Luther called such a life a *Beruf*, a calling, a vocation. This work ethic took the ideals of a monastic discipline and orderly life and moved it into worldly business. It led to the modern term "workaholic."

And here an interesting paradox emerges. There was a strong stress in this ascetical work ethic on frugality and the avoidance of luxurious living. But guess what? The harder you work, the better off you get; and the better off you get, the less appealing is frugality. This was a problem foreseen by John Wesley, the parent of Methodism. "I do not see how it is possible, in the nature of things, for any revival of true religion to continue long. For religion must necessarily produce both industry and frugality, and these cannot but produce riches. But as riches increase, so will pride, anger, and the love of the world in all its branches." Wesley had it right. Capitalism was fueled to a great extent by this religiously motivated work ethic, and lots of folks became rich. This led to a turn of the road. Since riches were the fruit of good Calvinist hard work and saving, they must also be a mark of the favor of God. There was a stubborn old idea in Christian history—a really bad idea—that some people were predestined to hell no matter what they did. That is scary, and it would be awfully nice to have some reassurance that you are not one of the damned.

This led to what I call the sacramentality of wealth. Money became the sign that you were saved. Bishop Lawrence of Massachusetts put it simply: "In the long run, it is only to the man of morality that wealth comes. . . . Godliness is in league with riches." This idea moved into the secular culture as religious ideas usually do. Secretary of State John Hay said in nineteenth-century America: "That you have property is proof of industry and foresight on your part or your father's; that you have nothing is a judgment on your laziness and vices or on your improvidence. The world is a moral world: which it would not be if virtue and vice received the same rewards." Ouch! That really hurts, especially if you're poor. It's about as far as you can get from the Gospel's "blessed are the poor"! This is "blessed are the rich," not the Gospel's "woe to you rich"! If you're poor, you're not only down and out, but God doesn't like you!

So what started out a rigorous religious ethics of hard work eventually became a glorification of wealth. And it also became the soul of Western (and now Eastern) capitalism. Capitalism needed industrious workers and a worship of wealth and accumulation. That is the message of Weber's book. In Keller's words: "We glimpse how the formidable spiritual energies of reformation could be channeled so profitably—and with such unjust and unsustainable effect."

Good Protestant News

Keller, like the good Protestant she is, does not flinch from the hard work of confessing and analyzing the sin that is in us. All traditions could take lessons from her and the Protestant tradition. There is a Buddhist saying that every belief system is an illness waiting to be cured. That is a bit overstated, but it has a message, since all religions are subject to corruption. But the upper side of confession is reform, and Protestants were born of the Reformation.

The analysis of the antinature work ethic was not the whole Protestant story, even though its influence was enormous. Another stress in Protestantism is *the book;* Protestantism is biblical. The book was not antinature. Keller notes: "Jesus the Nazarene seems to focus on what by later Christian standards seems subspiritual: feed the hungry, clothe the naked, visit the imprisoned, heal the sick." His parables drew from nature and the chores of daily life. As Keller puts it, Jesus "did not send us to our jobs on time, but rather back to the fragrant lilies!" And he took the time to point out approvingly that the lilies did not have the work ethic; "they neither toil nor spin" (Matt. 6:28). The birds also were not workaholics: "they neither sow nor reap nor gather into barns." And he added words that would make compulsive capitalists shriek: "So do not worry about tomorrow, for tomorrow will bring worries of its own" (Matt. 6:34).

Significantly, some of the best ecological ethics written by religious scholars today is written by Protestant biblical scholars like Catherine Keller, Larry Rasmussen, Dieter Hessel, James Nash, John Cobb, Sally McFague, James Martin-Schramm, and many more. Every religion is a work in progress. The best ingredients are there to correct the nasty missteps that all religions take. Keller points out that the fundamentalists in all of Christianity love to stress those parts of scripture that elevate Jesus' status while ignoring those parts that give his moral teaching. She is correct in this. Those references to the New Testament raised on banners behind the goalposts at football games we see on TV never refer to texts on feeding the hungry and visiting the prisoners, loving our enemies or offering one cheek when the other is struck by an attacker. It is easier to praise Jesus' stature than to take up the cross of commitment to the poor and follow him.

Protestant biblical scholarship has led the way into a modern reformation in Christianity. Catholic biblical scholarship started playing catch-up in the last fifty years. Jewish scholars now join with Christians in recovering the moral core of biblical religion. As the message gets out again, Keller points out, it is not surprising that many of the world's poorest and most exploited, from Tienanmen Square to the barrios of Latin America, are claiming Christianity as their own—and as their inspiration for liberation and decolonization.

Protestants have also been the first to shake off what we might call the "natalist" pro-fertility bias of Christianity against family planning. James Martin-Schramm offers the gift of criticism to the Catholic hierarchy on this:

> Vatican policies which proscribe artificial means of contraception must be critically challenged in the light of the effects of population growth on poverty and environmental degradation. These "prolife" policies are ambiguous at best since they certainly contribute to an increase in unwanted pregnancies which have a deleterious effect on the lives of poor women, their families, and the environment.

Christianity has proved its power to change the world and still does so. As I mentioned above, historian Garry Wills writes, most of the important moral movements that transformed America, "abolitionism, women's suffrage, the union movement, and the civil rights movement . . . grew out of religious circles." And we can add that they grew mainly out of Protestant religious circles.

The healthy and hopeful movements in Catholic liberation theology will be the topic of our final chapter.

12. Catholic Liberation Theology

THE CATHOLIC CHURCH IS CHANGING. That should be no surprise. That which lives, changes, and the Catholic Church is not dead. As our guide on Protestant Christianity, Catherine Keller, says, Christianity in all its forms represents "an immense, multilayered, self-contradicting unfinished field" of beliefs and practices. It is always remaking itself, always unfinished. *Ecclesia semper reformanda* is an old axiom of Christianity; it means that the church is *always* in need of reform.

Some years ago, I attended a conference in Mexico City. I spoke there with Catholic women from all over Latin America. The stories they told me pierced my soul and wet my eyes. One example: they told me about how in their countries they delayed baptism until the child was five or six years old. The reason? They had redefined the meaning of baptism. So many of their children died before that age, that when a child reached that age and appeared healthy enough to survive, the baptism became a celebration of thanksgiving that this child might be strong enough to live. From this experience of a poverty that we in the overconsuming rich world do not know, a new theology has appeared, and its impact is slowly spreading in many parts of Catholicism. It is called liberation theology.

In looking at this new theology and this ongoing Catholic reformation, our principal guide is Alberto Munera, S.J., a Jesuit priest living in the Dominican Republic. He sees his church and global capitalism from the vantage point of someone in the poor world. As he puts it: "I live in the Third World and I see the results daily of this lethal savagery that is blithely called 'the global economy.'" Father Munera asserts that his church is in the process of a major reform. In this reform, he says, "the perennial challenge is to draw from the past a living theology that meets the needs of the present and the future." Cardinal Joseph Ratzinger has made the same point. He said: "The Church is not the petrification of what once was, but its living presence in every age. The Church's dimension is therefore the present and the future no less than the past."

Liberation theology has largely appeared from the poorest parts of the Catholic world, especially Latin America. There is nothing radical about it. As Munera says, it is simply trying "to take seriously the acceptance and following of Jesus." To do this, liberation theology establishes two principles. The first: start your theology with the real world. Study that world in all of its economic and political and ecological reality (as we did in the first chapters of this book), because, after all, it is in the real world of economics and politics that the main decisions are made about who eats and who goes hungry, who lives and who dies, whose children are fed and literate and whose are buried in poverty, and what elements of the earth will be destroyed. This task demands, Munera says, "careful analysis of specific, particular, and concrete situations." In other words, don't get caught up in scintillating abstractions and fine theories (as much theology does) while people are starving under your nose. The Gospels were called "good news for the poor," and liberation theology wants to take that seriously.

The second principle of this reformist theology flows from the first: study every problem from the perspective of the poor. Test every policy and every vote you cast with the needs of the poor in mind. In Munera's words:

> Throughout the entire history of God's self-manifestation, the divine predilection for the poor is evident. God decides to become a poor man, Jesus Christ, to preach the Gospel to the poor and to liberate them from all injustice and oppression (Luke 4:16-21; Isa. 61:1-2). This is why practicing theology according to this method supposes first of all following the poor Jesus, assuming his commitment to the liberation of the poor and oppressed. . . . Theology must offer solutions to the real problems of the people.

Get real! That is liberation theology's mandate to other theologians. Part of this theology's realism is recognizing that seeing through the needs of the poor is the precise antidote to the way a lot of theology has been done. Theology tended to see everything from the perspectives of the rich and the secure. Most theology in the Christian world has been done in the champagne glass where the top 20 percent of the world receives 82 percent of its income (see chapter 2). Liberation theology is coming from the stem of the glass where the poor are being squeezed.

The Piety Bypass

This approach is solidly scriptural. Self-interest is blinding. Many Christian theologians in Germany during the formation of Nazism and the unfolding of the Holocaust continued to spin their abstract theories about the nature of the Trinity and other abstruse matters. Mass was offered daily in the lovely Catholic village of Dachau as the trains lumbered noisily past on their way to the death camp. Incense from the Dachau church liturgies floated up to mingle in the air with the smoke of the murdered dead. What god could welcome that unholy commingling or call it worship?

Piety and theology are good at hiding from the inconvenient facts of life, and it is against this perversity that the Jewish and Christian Bibles and liberation theology scream their protest. Piety, indeed, is often the first refuge of scoundrels. And are we not back in Dachau now, going about our pious business while 1.3 billion people are burning to death in the ovens of absolute poverty and while the earth and air and water of this sweet planet are corrupted by our greed and abuse? Outside the theological libraries, genocide and ecocide are raging. Liberation theology asks us to go outside where it is happening and start our thinking there.

The Anger of Justice

Alberto Munera sees three major strengths in the Catholic tradition that can help with the contemporary problems of overconsumption by the well-off, population stress, and rational reproductive ethics. The first act of justice is analysis of the problem, and when Munera analyzes, he get mad. From his view among the poor, he says accusingly "that the cost of the prosperity of the few rich is the poverty and death of millions of the poor." The essential needs of people are the central focus of Catholic social justice theory, and he says the needs of people and the delicate biology of the planet have "no status in global capitalism." At most, these needs beget "cynical gestures." "Workers are brutalized by unjust 'austerity' requirements to meet our debts to the First-World rich." He indicts theWTO, the World Bank, and the IMF and their cruel use of their "incredible power" to conduct the "rape of the poor." He calls these organizations that serve the rich stupid, since by destroying our ecology for short-term gain, "they are sawing the limb on which they sit" as they "destroy God's earth."

His justice ideas are pure *sedaqah* theology. Small wonder that Jews, Catholics, Muslims, and Protestants conscious of social justice are banding together. They are all returning to the moral passions of the prophets of Israel, those ancient specialists in *sedaqah*. Catholic social theory always had a positive view of government, contrary to right-wing thinking. Says Munera: "In Catholic social justice theory, government is not an evil to be minimized. It is the prime agent of distributive justice. Its natural role is the furtherance of the common good and the protection of the powerless and the poor." The hatred of government on the right wing is at root a hatred of sharing, since government has the clout to prevent people from hoarding their wealth while children die. Biblically speaking, *government is the prime protector of the common good with a particular concern for the powerless and the poor.* That is not something to be hated by any noble spirit.

Munera also cites the value of the Catholic harmony between nature and grace. There was always some *fuga mundi* spirituality (emphasizing flight from the world), but Catholic Christianity had a strong tradition of seeing nature as the first grace. Says Munera: "This was a sensuous, nature-friendly approach that saw the whole world as a mirror of God." Clearly Father Munera is one of those "southern people" scorned by the cold Kierkegaard. Catholic liturgy embodied all the elements of nature: water, oil, wine, bread, salt, wax, metals, fire, ashes, incense, vestments, physical touching, music, stone, and glass. It was of the earth and earthy. Says Munera: "Creative, ecologically sensitive adaptations of Catholic liturgy could emphasize in new ways the closeness of the natural order to the reality of God." That would be very Catholic.

The Catholic Case for Moral Pluralism

Sadly, the richness of Catholic thought on social justice and its application to ecological ethics is generally unknown. Many people think that Catholic thought is obsessively focused on pelvic issues, on sexual and reproductive matters. On these matters, all that most people see is a bunch of pelvic taboos. No contraception. No abortion. No family planning. Obviously, that can make for some problems on a crowded earth. This blind alley is the fault of poor hierarchical teaching, since the Catholic tradition actually has a prochoice as well as a no-choice position even on the issue of abortion. Father Munera alludes to this openness but does not develop it—understandably. As a priest, he is under tight control by the Vatican.

Let me rehearse some of what I have written elsewhere to lend a little needed light on this moral controversy that obstructs population policy in countries like the United States as well as in the so-called Catholic countries.

Although it is virtually unknown even by modern Catholics, the Roman Catholic position on abortion is pluralistic. It has a strong prochoice tradition and a conservative antichoice tradition. Neither is official, and neither is more Catholic than the other. The hierarchical attempt to portray the Catholic position as univocal, an unchanging negative wafted through twenty centuries of untroubled consensus, is dissolved by a chastening walk through history and a little honest scholarship. By unearthing this perfectly orthodox openness to choice on abortion and on contraception in the core of the tradition, the status of the antichoice position is revealed as only one among many Catholic views.

The Bible does not condemn abortion. The closest it gets to it is in Exodus, which speaks of accidental abortion. This imposes a financial penalty on "people who are fighting" and cause a woman to miscarry (21:22). The patriarchal issue here is the father's right to progeny; he could fine you for the misdeed, but he could not claim "an eye for an eye" as if *a person* had been killed. Thus, as conservative theologian John Connery, S.J., said, "the fetus did not have the same status as the mother in Hebrew Law."

Following on the virtual silence of Scripture on abortion, the early church history treats it only incidentally and sporadically. Indeed, there is no systematic study of the question until the fifteenth century. The early references to abortion do not constitute a condemnation of abortion as homicide but as part of behavior that frustrates the procreative purpose of sex. They proceeded from the belief that sperm consisted of *homunculi,* little human beings, some of whom would grow into full-grown babies in the womb, the mother providing only the locus. Thus, at times in the early centuries, male masturbation was described as homicide. One early church writer, Tertullian, discusses what we would today call a late-term emergency abortion where doctors had to dismember a fetus in order to remove it, and he refers to this emergency measure as a *crudelitas necessaria,* a "necessary cruelty." Obviously, this amounted to moral permission of abortion in a conflict situation.

One thing that develops early on and becomes the dominant tradition in Christianity is the theory of delayed animation or ensoulment. Borrowed from the Greeks, this taught that the spiritual human soul did not arrive in the fetus until as late as three months into the pregnancy. Prior to that time, whatever life was there was not *personal.* They opined that the embryo was enlivened first by a vegetative soul, then an animal soul, and only when formed sufficiently, by a human spiritual soul at about three months into the pregnancy. The early fetus did not have the status of *person,* nor would killing it fit the category of murder, since murder is by definition *the unjust killing of a person.*

This idea of delayed ensoulment survived throughout the tradition. Saint Thomas Aquinas, the most esteemed of medieval theologians, held to this view. Thus, the most traditional and stubbornly held position in Catholic Christianity is that early abortions are not murder. Since the vast number of abortions done today in the United States, for example, are early abortions, they are not, according to this Catholic tradition, murder. Also, all pregnancy terminations done through the use of the more recently available abortifacient RU 486 would not qualify as the killing of a human person according to this tradition of delayed ensoulment. Properly and honestly understood, the Catholic tradition is not as obtuse and unnuanced as conservative Catholics, bishops, popes, and other Christians would portray it.

In the fifteenth century, the saintly Dominican archbishop of Florence, Antoninus, was the first to do extensive work on abortion. He approved of early abortions to save the life of the woman, a class with many members in the primitive context of fifteenth-century medicine. This became common teaching. Archbishop Antoninus was not criticized by the Vatican for his prochoice position. Indeed, he was later canonized as a saint. (Catholic bishops today might well begin their discussions of abortion with a prayer to Saint Antoninus.) When an opinion like this is expressed without exciting any ruckus, it is a signal that the view was already common and was merely being clearly expressed.

In the sixteenth century, the influential Antoninus de Corduba said that medicine that was abortifacient could be taken *even later in a pregnancy* if required for the health of the mother. The mother, he insisted, had a *jus prius,* a "prior right." Some of the maladies he discussed do not seem to have been a matter of life and death for the women, and yet he allows that abortifacient medicine even in these cases is morally permissible. Jesuit theologian Thomas Sanchez, who died in the early seventeenth century, said that all of his contemporary Catholic theologians approved of early abortion to save the life of the woman. None of these theologians or bishops was censured for these views. Their limited prochoice position was considered thoroughly orthodox. It has been said that conservatives are the worshipers of dead liberals! Part of their affliction, obviously, is amnesia.

In the nineteenth century, as improved communications were promoting centralization in Roman Catholicism, the Vatican was invited to enter a debate on a very-late-term abortion, requiring dismemberment of a formed fetus in

order to save the woman's life. On September 2, 1869, the
Vatican refused to decide the case. It referred the questioner
to the teaching of theologians on the issue. It was, in other
words, the business of the theologians to discuss it freely and
arrive at a conclusion. It was not for the Vatican to decide.
This appropriate modesty and disinclination to intervene in
legitimate theological debate is an older and wiser Catholic
model.

What this brief history shows is that there is ambiguity
and pluralism in the Catholic theological tradition on abortion. The twentieth-century absolutism, in which abortion
gradually came to be seen as "intrinsically evil," is a novelty.
Clearly, something else is in play. The sudden onset of such
rigidity must hide some other power agenda, and I suggest
that it relates to the rise of women starting in the nineteenth
century. At any rate, Vatican theology today, in what I have
described as the pelvic turn in Catholic thought, gives a
prominence in the definition of orthodoxy to issues of sexual
and reproductive ethics that is not typical of the Christian
tradition in healthier moments.

This hierarchical obsession with the abortion and contraception issues poorly serves the Catholic tradition and its
powerful social justice tradition. Father Munera points out
that there are great and sensitive things taught by the popes
and the Vatican Council of bishops on care for the poor, on
critiques of the evils of capitalism as well as communism, on
the need to forgive the debts of poor nations, on the obligation to cherish the earth which is God's creation, and more.
These helpful and courageous hierarchical and papal teachings tend to get ignored because of the distorting obsession of
a conservative hierarchy with issues of sexual and reproductive ethics, issues on which good people for good reasons
may and do respectfully disagree. It is insulting to other
world religions to treat their more liberal views on family
planning as indefensible. The Religious Consultation on
Population, Reproductive Health and Ethics, which was the
ground on which this book grew, is developing another project named the Right to Family Planning, Contraception, and
Abortion in Ten World Religions. The project will show pro-

choice positions alongside no-choice positions on abortion in all these religions. When so many good people see things differently, a little humility on the part of the Vatican would help.

"Conscientizing" Capitalism

Finally, Alberto Munera shows that liberation theology is not a whimsical dream trip. He doesn't expect the capitalist system to disappear and be replaced by a kind of democratic socialism that would end poverty and be a lot closer to the biblical ideal. He concedes that "the fact remains: we are within a capitalist system and we move within capitalist structures." His goal is "to socialize capitalism and bring conscience to it. . . . The challenge is to mitigate and conscientize (a new term frequently used by liberation theologians) capitalism." Maybe, he says, this gargantuan ambition could be realized if the "vigorous spiritualities" of the world's religions can unite as they are doing in this book, "to confront uncontrolled population growth, overconsumption, and ecological disaster."

This delightful and courageous man embodies the new look of Roman Catholicism. His biblically grounded vision of morality is a bridge to all the religions of the world. Deep down, all of them are responses of awe and appreciation for the miracle of life on earth. Their attention to the essential needs of this earth is belated but rich in promise.

Conclusion

CHANGING THIS WORLD MIGHT SEEM HOPELESS. It is not. Laurie Zoloth writes of how the rabbis writing when Rome ruled the world might have thought it impossible to have any impact against overwhelming power. She wrote: "Rome controlled and defined the entire world known to the scholars writing under its yoke. Their ability to dominate the environment must have seemed as total as the economy of the multinational economy does to us today." It didn't stop them, nor can we be stopped. Only despair can stop us.

The first Earth Day in the United States thirty years ago seemed a hopeless gesture. It wasn't. It planted a seed, as other seeds were being planted throughout the world. One result is the United States Environmental Protection Agency where every day is Earth Day. Another was the 1992 world summit in Rio de Janeiro, Brazil, the largest assembly of nations dedicated to the protection of the earth. The war in Vietnam seemed unstoppable until the people caught on, and then they stopped it. Communism seemed omnipotent until the people caught on, and then they stopped it.

The religions of the world are great symphonies of hope. And hope gets things done.

When Israel started, it was unthinkable that there could be government of the people, by the people, for the people. The king or pharaoh was the image of God, and there was no power greater than the divine right of kings. The Israelite reformers turned that around and said, Do you want to see the image of God? Don't go to the castle. Look instead at the baby sleeping in my arms. There is the image of God. Look at my grandfather there by the fire. His mind is not as clear as it once was, but he is the image of God. And go to the reflecting pond and look at that simple face looking back at you. You are looking at the image of God! This was a revolution that shook the economics and politics of the world. It was the beginning of democratic theory and the eventual undermining of royalty.

Buddhism moved into Tibet, where the ideal of every young man was to be a warrior. When it took root, the ideal of young men was to be monks dedicated to peace. When Patrick brought biblical religion to Ireland, the adornment of young men were strings of skulls, badges of their killing prowess. When this religious revolution was over, those same men carried scrolls that they had copied as the love of education replaced the love of war. In modern times, the people of Kerala, one of the poorest states in India, became inflamed with the love of learning. They proved that ideas embraced by an educated people can transform society against the worst odds.

In many parts of the world, microloans are being given to women who are starting small cottage businesses, and the repayment rate for these loans would make first-world bankers green with envy.

Never underestimate the power of a good idea.

An ideal is an idea on fire. Religions are hotbeds of ideals and common sense. Solidarity with all that lives, compassion for the weakest among us, delight in the gift of life—all are themes that run through all the religions studied in this volume. All these religions stress that *owing* is at least as important as *owning*. What we *owe* to other humans and to all the rest of nature is more important than our ability to grab a little bit of earth and *own* it. Gratitude does more for the earth and society than does acquisition. Indigenous North American religions always begin their rituals with thanks. There is basic wisdom in that. Ingratitude may even be seen as the root of all evil. The great Jewish theologian Abraham Heschel said that humankind will not die for lack of information, but it may die for lack of appreciation.

What the earth needs is a rebirth of awe and wonder and gratitude, the best of human emotions, and the source of those phenomena we call religions. If we recover our sense of the sacredness of the gift of life and get recharged with the electricity of ideals and delight, the ongoing destruction can abate and the bare, ruined choirs of planet earth can sing again. To paraphrase the Irish poet William Butler Yeats, that may be only a dream, but tread softly, very softly, if you tread upon that dream!

A Brief Annotated Bibliography

Note: All of the books listed are available in paperback.

Visions of a New Earth: Religious Perspectives on Population, Consumption, and Ecology, edited by Harold Coward and Daniel C. Maguire (SUNY Press, 2000), is the work on which *Sacred Energies* is largely based. In it you meet the authors to whom you were introduced in this book speaking in their own voices.

Population, Consumption, and the Environment: Religious and Secular Responses, edited by Harold Coward (SUNY Press, 1995), contains essays on the various world religions, some of them by authors you have met in *Sacred Energies.*

The World's Religions: Our Great Wisdom Traditions, by Huston Smith (Harper & Row, 1991), is a beautifully written introduction to the world's religions.

Feminism and World Religions, edited by Arvind Sharma and Katherine K. Young (SUNY Press, 1999), is another multireligion book discussing the fundamental changes brought about by feminism in all the world religions.

Christianity and Ecology: Seeking the Well-Being of Earth and Humans, edited by Dieter T. Hessel and Rosemary Radford Ruether (Harvard University Press, 2000), is part of a series of volumes, each concentrating on one of the world religions and its treatment of ecology and reverence for the environment.

How Many People Can the Earth Support? by Joel E. Cohen (Norton, 1995), is the most thorough and respected study in recent years on the actual state of the world and all of its resources.

A Green History of the World: The Environment and the Collapse of Great Civilizations, by Clive Ponting (Penguin, 1992), is a remarkable study of how humans have treated the world and the ideas and attitudes that affect our behavior.

Ethics for a Small Planet, by Daniel C. Maguire and Larry L. Rasmussen (SUNY Press, 1998), is a short book that diagnoses the human condition and offers prospects for life on this planet.

Index

133